HANNAH CHAN

By Glenda Hofmann

Copyright ©2013 by Glenda Hofmann
ISBN: 978-0-9920906-0-9

Cover photo by Father

All rights reserved. No part of the this publication may be reproduced, stored in a retrieval system, or transmitted in any form or by any means, electronic, mechanical, photocopying, recording or otherwise, without the prior permission of the publisher.

Contents

Preface 5
Chapter 1 A Visit To Iwagi Shogakko 9
Chapter 2 Off To School 15
Chapter 3 Iwagijima—A Tiny Island 19
Chapter 4 A Hanka And A Napukin 21
Chapter 5 At The Beach 25
Chapter 6 Mother's Daily Duties 31
Chapter 7 Kyuushoku—Lunchtime At Iwagi Shogakko 35
Chapter 8 Fishing In Iwagijima 39
Chapter 9 Canada Day 43
Chapter 10 Ofuro—The Bath 47
Chapter 11 Lunch At Macdonald's 49
Chapter 12 The Telephone 55
Chapter 13 Bugs At Night 59
Chapter 14 Crabs 63
Chapter 15 Cleaners 69
Chapter 16 A Surprise For Taro And Hannah 71
Chapter 17 School Days 75
Chapter 18 Computer Class 79
Chapter 19 Lemonade And Wheelchairs 81

Chapter 20 Very Old People ... 85
Chapter 21 Getting Ready For Swimming Lessons ... 89
Chapter 22 Swimming Lessons ... 93
Chapter 23 Early Morning Deliveries ... 97
Chapter 24 Taro And Hannah ... 103
Chapter 25 Fruit Picking ... 107
Chapter 26 The Thermos ... 113
Chapter 27 Bosses For The Day ... 117
Chapter 28 Taro's Fight ... 119
Chapter 29 Kuru Kuru Sushi ... 125
Chapter 30 The Secret ... 131
Chapter 31 Big Flush / Small Flush ... 137
Chapter 32 Catching Dragonflies ... 141
Chapter 33 The Good Bye Speech ... 149
Chapter 34 Last Day Of School ... 153
Chapter 35 Neon Lights ... 157
Chapter 36 Sayonara, Ikedasan ... 165
Chapter 37 Leaving Iwagijima ... 169
About the Author ... 175

PREFACE

The parents in this story were from small towns on Canada's west coast. Following graduate school in London they moved together to Singapore, where Father began a new job teaching law at the national university. After his contract had finished they moved to Hong Kong and three years later Mother was offered a position teaching language and literature at Japan's oldest women's university. This time Father followed Mother and they set up a small house in Tokyo.

Adopting a child in Japan is not difficult if one of the parents speaks Japanese. Mother and Father applied to the municipal adoption agency and to a private Catholic adoption agency and were thoroughly vetted by both. The private agency telephoned first, and Mother and Father took Taro home on 24 hours' notice. He was 10 days old. A short time later, as so often happens, Mother became pregnant. Not long after that the municipal agency called to ask whether they would like to adopt a small boy. With one infant at home and another one on the way, Mother and Father decided to decline the offer.

Meanwhile Father, whose languages did not include Japanese, decided that it would be better for him if Mother delivered her baby in a Canadian hospital. And so the family moved back to Vancouver three months before Hannah was born.

HANNAH CHAN

Although Taro and Hannah were raised in a Vancouver suburb theirs was not a typical Canadian childhood. Mother did all that she could to fulfill her promise to the adoption agency that she would teach Taro about his ethnic and cultural heritage. This was not at all a burden for her. As a trained anthropologist she saw it as an opportunity for adventure. In fact, as soon as Hannah was born, Mother set a plan into motion. She advertised in the local Japanese newspaper for a 'mother's helper.' Her idea was that in exchange for a few days of help each week the helper would receive free room and board, a little spending money and the opportunity to experience life in a Canadian family. The most important part of her plan was not so much being able to receive some help but rather for Taro, Hannah and herself to be immersed in the Japanese language. The first helpers were such great successes that when Mother went back to work a year after Hannah was born she hired a Japanese nanny full time.

In the eight years following Hannah's birth Mother invited six young Japanese women, one after the other, to live in the family's suite downstairs. They were nurses or teachers or childcare workers. Most of the women came on working holiday visas; one was so special that she stayed for four years and Mother and Father sponsored her to live in Canada permanently.

The only rule in the house was that the Japanese women would never speak English to the children. They never considered speaking anything but Japanese with Mother. Taro and Hannah quickly learned to categorize people by language. With the Japanese women they would speak only Japanese. With Mother, they were happy to speak in either English or Japanese. With Father however, they insisted on English. Whenever Father tried to speak Japanese with Taro and Hannah they would get angry, cover their ears and yell *"Dame*—bad! No Japanese!"

PREFACE

Over the years many Japanese women lived in Canada with Taro and Hannah's family. Their names were Toshiko, Sumiko, Kumiko, Yuki, Yumi, Rumi, Nozomi and Aika. But this story came about because of a young woman named Sachiko. Sachiko had worked as a nurse in Kobe before coming to Vancouver. She had grown up on a very small island in the Japan Inland Sea. Sometimes when she and Mother sat down for tea Sachiko would reminisce about the experiences of her childhood. Mother enjoyed her stories so much that when Sachiko invited the whole family to visit her island Mother readily accepted. Sachiko contacted her old primary school principal to ask if it might be possible for Taro and Hannah to attend school on the island. When Naka-moto sensei replied that the children would be welcome at Iwagi Shogakko, Sachiko's parents set about finding a house for the family to rent, and soon Mother, Father, Taro and Hannah were on their way to Iwagijima for the start of the next school term.

CHAPTER 1

A VISIT TO IWAGI SHOGAKKO

"Mom, wait! They won't stay on. They're too big! They keep falling off—wait!" Hannah curled up her toes as tightly as she could in the big plastic slippers. She began sliding her way down the hall towards the principal's office. Everyone was hurriedly shuffling about and bowing and speaking in Japanese. Hannah's father was bowing too, and saying *'domo domo,'* as he always did in these kinds of situations. Hannah sat down beside her brother Taro. She picked up the glass that had been placed in front of her, sniffed at it, and took a small, tentative sip. 'Yuck' she thought to herself, *mugi-cha*—cold barley tea'. She watched as Taro picked up his cup and drank it all down. "Aren't you thirsty, Hannah?" he said.

❦

"You must be Hannah chan. I am Nakamoto and this is Ikeuchi sensei and Miyamoto sensei. Welcome to Iwagi Shogakko," said the older lady with greying hair. "Miyamoto sensei will be your teacher, Hannah chan. And Taro kun, your teacher will be Ikeuchi sensei."

Both teachers smiled and bowed and said a few words to the children in Japanese. Hannah smiled shyly. Her face started to redden. A whole group of children had gathered in the doorway. They were talking and giggling and pushing their way in to get a good look at Hannah and Taro.

"*Hannah chan kawaii ne*—Hannah is cute isn't she? *Taro kun ookii ne*—look at how big Taro is," they said. Hannah glanced up at the children and then quickly looked away. Taro kept his eyes on the floor. Nakamoto sensei, the principal of Iwagi Elementary School, was passing out forms to Mother and going over all the things that needed to be done before Hannah and Taro could start school.

"We are very happy to have Hannah chan and Taro kun at our school," said Nakamoto sensei in Japanese. "It is our first time to do such a thing. We hope that Hannah chan and Taro kun will learn many things about Iwagi and about Japan. We hope also that our Iwagi children will learn many things about children and school in Canada from Taro kun and Hannah chan. Let's share our cultures. It will be a good experience for both," she said.

Mother and Father smiled, bowed their heads and said '*domo arigato*' to Nakamoto sensei. And although Nakamoto sensei directed her comments to both Mother and Father equally, it was Mother, as always, who responded. Father followed the conversation as best he could but seldom spoke. The children meanwhile, relying on their mother, thought of other things.

It was kind of scary, going to school in Japan, thought Hannah to herself. And it was all because of Taro, her older brother, who had been adopted from Japan as a baby. It wasn't fair that she had to get dragged along too. She knew it wasn't really his fault though. He couldn't speak Japanese any better than she could. And he didn't much know what was going on either. 'I bet he's a little scared too,' she thought. After all, he had spent almost his whole life in West Vancouver, not Japan. Hannah wished she were back in Canada now, with her friends at school. She understood everything there. Not like now.

Nakamoto sensei continued: "There are some rules we will ask you to follow. Please come to school on time. Hannah and Taro, a group of children who live nearby will come to collect you tomorrow morning at seven thirty. Please be ready. You must wear your uniform. Any T-shirt is okay to wear but, *sssssaaaaaa,* not a bright colour, not like this one Taro kun is wearing today. Hannah chan, yours is okay."

Mother looked a little confused. Taro was wearing a red and blue T-shirt and Hannah was wearing a lime green T-shirt. Mother asked for clarification. "Nakamoto sensei…. so red is not a good colour for school?" she asked.

"No, no, it is too bright, it is distracting for study," replied Nakamoto sensei.

Mother continued… "So which colours are okay to wear? Is blue alright?" asked Mother.

"Yes, yes, blue is fine, or white or black…"

"How about orange," asked Mother.

"No, no, orange is too bright. No bright colours," responded Nakamoto.

Mother, a little perplexed, pointed at Hannah's neon lime green T-shirt.

"Yes, it is fine," said Nakamoto sensei.

Mother quickly ran through her mind, the few T-shirts that she had packed for the children and asked, "yellow?"

"Yes, of course yellow is fine to wear. Only bright colours are against the rules because they are distracting," she repeated.

Mother smiled. "Yes, I understand," she said.

"Also, shoes," said Nakamoto sensei. "The children need both outdoor shoes and indoor shoes to wear'.

"Yes, we have those," said Mother.

Nakamoto sensei walked over to a table beside the window. She picked up a stack of books and returned. "Here are your text books,

Hannah chan," said Nakamoto sensei as she placed the colourful paperback books on the table in front of her. "You are eight. You will be a third grade student. And Taro kun, you are nine, you will be a fourth grade student. Here are yours".

"*Arigato, arigato,*" said Taro and Hannah in unison.

Miyamoto sensei, Hannah's teacher, opened one of Hannah's texts in front of her and asked in Japanese: "Hannah chan, can you read any of this?" Hannah looked carefully at the text and began to read slowly. Everyone in the room went quiet. "*Sugoi, sugoi*—wow! Hannah chan can read," remarked Miyamoto sensei. Taro, also was asked to read and again the teachers were surprised that he could.

The meeting ended with more bowing and with Mother and Father backing slowly out of Nakamoto sensei's office, bowing and saying *"domo, domo"*.

Later that afternoon, at home, Hannah and Taro spread out their things for school on the tatami mat floor. There were colourful new text books but the rest of the supplies had been borrowed from here and there. Some were clean and new. Others were worn and tatty.

"That school bag is mine," said Hannah, claiming the cleaner, less worn of the two yellow backpacks. "It has red trim. Red is for girls. Taro, yours is the one with black." Hannah opened the pack, looked in, swished her hand around and then closed it. She examined the small pink teddy bear key chain dangling from the front flap. She looked at all the school things on the floor: pencils, crayons, notebooks. There were two long wooden paint brushes for doing Japanese calligraphy. There were white gowns with caps and white masks that covered the mouth and nose and looped around the ears. Hannah picked these up and put them on. "Look, Mom," she said. "I'm a doctor."

A VISIT TO IWAGI SHOGAKKO

Taro looked up. "Those are for *kyuushoku*—lunchtime, stupid," he said.

"Don't say 'stupid' to your sister," said Father.

"I think I'll wear this for Hallowe'en," said Hannah.

"Yaa," said Taro. "You can be Dr. Frankenstein!"

Taro picked up a well worn yellow cap and put it on. "What do you think, Mom?" he asked.

"That looks great, Taro! Why don't you guys try on the rest of your stuff, see if it fits," said Mother.

"Those shorts look way too small," said Taro

"Yaaa, well look at my skirt! It's humungous!" retorted Hannah.

"Just try them on, you might be surprised," said Mother. Taro and Hannah put on their uniforms.

"These look stupid!" said Taro, looking down at his bare legs. "It looks like I don't have any pants on." His long brown jacket covered his buttocks as well as the short shorts he was wearing. "Boy, am I glad none of my Canadian friends can see me like this!" he said.

Hannah slipped into her skirt. "Oh my gosh, Mom, I *can't* wear this!" protested Hannah. The pleated brown skirt came nearly down to her ankles and was far too wide at the waist. It hung like a hula hoop around her middle held up by suspenders over her shoulders.

"Well... how about the jacket. Put that on," said Mother. "See, that looks good. That fits."

"I guess the jacket is okay. But look, some of the buttons are missing and it's all splattered with paint and, and what about the skirt, I *can't* wear the skirt. What am I going to do? Everyone will have a skirt and I won't. I will get into trouble. The kids will all look at me and, and…"

Mother quickly interjected. "Don't worry, Hannah. Tomorrow you can wear your jacket with a pair of shorts. You can bring back the skirt and show them. I'm sure someone can find a skirt to fit you."

HANNAH CHAN

"Are you sure?" asked Hannah.
"I promise," said Mother.

Iwagi Shogakko (elementary school)

CHAPTER 2

OFF TO SCHOOL

The next morning Mother got the children up early. She laid out their clothes on the tatami floor and put out breakfast on the low table.

"Are they here yet?" asked Hannah. "What time are they coming?"

"No, no, you have lots of time. You have thirty minutes before they get here," answered Mother.

"I'm not very hungry," said Hannah.

"Oh, oh can I have it, can I have yours," asked Taro reaching across the table to take Hannah's scrambled eggs.

"No Taro; just leave it please," said Mother. "Hannah, try to eat a little, okay? It's good to have something in your stomach before school."

"I don't want any. I'm not hungry!" said Hannah.

Taro clicked through the channels on the TV. "Wow, this TV is really bad, there is nothing on," he said.

"That's okay, Taro, why don't you grab a book and sit outside where you can watch for them."

"Can I play Gameboy … please?"

"Well, alright, but you'll have to turn it off as soon as you see the kids coming—okay?"

"Gotcha!" replied Taro.

Hannah and Taro sat outside on the step in front of their small house and waited. There were cats everywhere. Hannah went up to a kitten, and reached out to pet it, but Mother quickly stopped her. "No, Hannah, don't encourage them," said Mother.

"Why not?" asked Hannah.

"Look at that one," said Mother. She pointed to a tiny tabby kitten with an oozing eye. "And that one... look, its back leg is covered in open sores. If you pet them you might catch something. Besides, they'll keep coming over and we don't want that. Remember, Mrs. Ikeda warned us not to be friendly with the cats."

❦

Soon three children in yellow hats and brown school uniforms could be seen at the top of the narrow lane. One boy was carrying a small yellow flag.

"They're here, Mom," called Hannah. "Can you help me get my backpack on? she asked. Mother helped Hannah put on the heavy pack, which was bulging with extra shoes, a thermos and all of the new textbooks and supplies.

"It should be lighter tomorrow," said Mother. "Just remember to leave your books and shoes at school."

"*Ohayo gozaimasu*—good morning," called out the children.

"*Ohayo*," replied Taro and Hannah. They took up their positions at the rear of the group and waved goodbye, following a few steps behind the other children.

"Oh, I hope they'll be alright," said Mother.

"They'll be fine," said Father.

OFF TO SCHOOL

School uniforms

View from the mountain top of Iwagijima

CHAPTER 3

IWAGIJIMA–A TINY ISLAND

Iwagijima is a tiny island in the Japan Inland Sea. There is one main road around the island, and a bus which circles the island a few times each day. The bus is free. Most of the passengers on the bus are elderly folk making their way to the supermarket or seniors' center. Everyone else gets around the island by mini cars or bicycles.

There is a Co-op supermarket and a post office. There is a small store called Emi Fashion and a tiny shoe store selling very basic footwear. There is a hairdresser, a barbershop and a library. Finally, there is a Farmer's Co-op bank and a hardware store, a mechanic and a bicycle repair shop. These few stores and services sell or do very little. In fact, most Iwagi islanders hop on the ferries once a week to do their shopping at larger stores on larger islands.

Every few days, a travelling salesman arrives at the port to set up his wares near the centre of town. Sometimes, it will be a 'sewing man,' who lays out his threads and needles and buttons and bolts of cloth on tables for all the passers by to see. Sometimes, the 'gum boot and shoe man' comes, arranging his baskets of boots and shoes on the sidewalks. Mother's favourite was the '*bonsai* man' who would come and set up a grand selection of miniature trees: beautiful blossoming trees, and ancient, sculpted pines in ceramic containers the size of dinner plates. And though daily shopping was a bit of a novelty for Mother it was not always easy to do.

Father in the streets of Iwagi

CHAPTER 4

A HANKA AND A NAPUKIN

Mother and Father could hear footsteps and children's voices in the narrow lane outside of their house. Father hurried to the door. "Taro kun, Hannah chan, how was school?"

Mother quickly rushed to the children to help them with their back packs and to unload their belongings in the *genkan*—entry hall. "How was your first day?" she asked.

"Oh Mom, they were *soooo* nice to me. I couldn't believe it! Look, look at all the stuff I got. Look, Mom." Hannah dug through her back pack and pulled out a long colourful paper chain necklace and draped it around her neck. "They made this for me. I had to stand up at the front of the class and all the kids came up to me one by one and read me something that they had written. It was so much fun!"

Hannah showed Mother all of the letters she had received. Each was beautifully written in *hiragana* and neatly folded into envelopes which were decorated with colourful stickers.

"So… maybe school won't be so bad here after all," said Mother.

"And look, I got a new skirt. Nami chan's mother found a better size for me."

"It looks great, Hannah," said Mother. "How was your day, Taro?"

"It was pretty good… look, I got some letters too!" Taro held out a handful of envelopes for Mother to see. "The teacher's pretty nice but the boys are kind of wild and noisy and they fool around a lot."

"Oh well, maybe they're just excited to have a new kid in their class," said Mother.

"Yaa, maybe," said Taro. "Oh Mom, we've GOT to have a *hanka* and a *napukin* for tomorrow and we need to carry a package of tissues in our pockets."

"You need a what?" asked Mother

"A *hanka* and a *napukin*," said Taro and Hannah together.

"Oh, well, what exactly is a *hanka* and a *napukin*?" asked Mother.

Hannah quickly jumped in, "Well, a *hanka*, it's kind of like a small cloth square and you keep it in your pocket. When you wash your hands after using the washroom you dry them with the *hanka*. There's no paper towels Mom, in the washroom," explained Hannah.

"Oh I see"… said Mother, "You mean a handkerchief."

"Huh," said Taro. "No, no, it's not that. It's a *hanka*."

"Oh Mom, we also need a *napukin*," said Hannah.

"What does that look like?" asked Mother.

"Well, it's like this big square of cloth," explained Taro.

"Is it the same size as the *hanka*," asked Mother.

"Well, not exactly. It's bigger and thicker and you put it on your desk when you eat your lunch," said Hannah.

"Exactly!" said Taro. "And we've got to have it by tomorrow."

"Well," said Mother. "I will check in the supermarket and the Co-op and see what I can find."

A HANKA AND A NAPUKIN

Hannah's class Miyamoto-sensei

Taro's class Ikeuchi-sensei

CHAPTER 5

AT THE BEACH

Before dinner Mother, Father, Taro and Hannah went out exploring. Iwagijima was a very old island. Villagers had been living on the island for more than six hundred years. There were Shinto shrines and Buddhist temples everywhere. Some were very old with ancient, crumbling roofs and walls. Others looked quite new with fresh scented wooden buildings, charming pathways and lovely gardens.

On occasion, islanders could be seen tending the graves of their ancestors. More often, though, the temple grounds were empty and were a great place to play. There were beautiful old bells to ring with ropes or poles. There were long stone staircases leading to hill top temples, and bridges to ponds with *koi* swimming. People didn't seem to mind Taro and Hannah running about or playing Hide and Seek in and out of the narrow paths and gravestones.

After awhile, Mother went off on her bicycle to do the shopping. Father and the children wandered down to the sea. The paths and alleys all seemed to lead down to the ocean or up to the hills. Hannah loved going to the seashore. There was a breeze there and it wasn't so stiflingly hot.

There were always lots of treasures to find, too. The shells were more interesting than the ones she could get back at home in Vancouver. Father had even bought her a book in Tokyo, which helped her to identify them. The sand was soft and white and felt good between her toes and the water was clear. Even though it was not yet swimming season in Japan and Hannah had been told not to go in the water, compared with May in Canada the weather felt very, very hot to Taro and Hannah. Hannah could not resist dipping her feet into the cool water.

※

When the tide was way out, the islanders would come with their buckets and shovels to dig for clams and other shellfish. Hannah and Taro would peer into their buckets to see what they had caught.

"What do you do with those long ones?" Taro asked the *ojiisan*—grandfather, pointing to the cigar shaped shellfish. "Can you eat them?"

"Ah, yes; very tasty. They are razor clams. They are very delicious in soups."

Grandfathers and grandmothers would be digging away while young children dashed about searching for squirters. "Here's one, Grandfather," shouted a child pointing to a small hole in the sand which was squirting out a stream of water. Higher up on the sandy shore old, old women with hunched over bodies were collecting dried up seaweed. Hannah rushed here and there looking for interesting and colourful shells to put into her pail.

"Look Dad," Hannah yelled, holding up a small piece of broken pottery. "Do you think Mom would like this?" she asked. Father ran his thumb over the smooth surface carefully examining the piece.

"That's a beautiful one, Hannah, I think Mom would like it," he said. Mother had been collecting interesting fragments of pottery.

AT THE BEACH

She was hoping to make something with them when they returned to Canada.

As Iwagijima was a very old island and because the center of the island was a large mountain, it was quite common for all kinds of things to get washed down from the mountain tops to the sea shore. Some days Hannah could find tiny old coloured glass bottles or ornate ceramic roofing tiles with faces on them. There were always lots of pieces of broken pottery being washed down the mountain streams to the sea. If Hannah looked carefully on the pottery fragments she could find parts of a dragon, or a pine tree forest, a duck or a flower.

❦

"Taro, Hannah," yelled Mother from the street above. "Dinner will be ready soon. Let's go home." Mother sat on the concrete ledge above the sandy beach and waited while the children brushed off the sand from their feet and slipped into their sandals. "You're bringing all *that* home?" asked Mother, looking into Hannah's bucket. "Are you sure you need it all?"

"Yes, Mom, I need it for my collection!" said Hannah. Mother sighed. They had only been on Iwagi a short time and already the cupboard in their small Japanese house was filling up with container after container of bits of pottery, dried crabs and seashells.

"Mom!" protested Hannah, "I need them! What's for dinner anyway. I'm starving!"

Up ahead on the path, a stooped over old woman pushing a walker was moving slowly towards Mother, Father and the children.

"*Konnichiwa*—hello," she said. "I am the great aunt of Ikeda."

She gave a wide toothless smile and held out a big bag of onions.

"Here, these are for you," she said. "They are from my *hatake*—garden."

"*Sugoi!! Oishii so, arigato*—wow, they look delicious," said Mother, bowing and smiling to the old lady. Taro and Hannah also bowed and said, "*arigato.*" They continued along their way. When the old lady was out of earshot Hannah and Taro looked up at Mother. They both started to giggle.

"Mom, oh no, another bag of onions!" joked Hannah. "What are you going to do with them all?"

Mother and Father had been receiving boxes and bags of onions daily. There was not a lot of room in the small Japanese house and so Mother was placing them neatly on the wooden platform outside the sliding doors of the tatami mat room. Mother had been using up the onions as best she could, adding them to stir fries and to her *miso* soup. Father had even invented 'onion steaks,' but like the seashells in the cupboard, the piles of onions were growing bigger and bigger.

Another bag of onions!

AT THE BEACH

Mother and Mrs. Furumura

CHAPTER 6

MOTHER'S DAILY DUTIES

The next morning, Taro and Hannah were up early. They had finished breakfast and Mother was packing their school bags. "What would you like to take to drink in your thermos?" asked Mother.

"We're supposed to take tea or water," said Hannah.

"Yaa, but I don't like drinking tea or water," complained Taro.

"Me neither," said Hannah.

"Well, how about I put in some juice for you? No one will be able to see, so you should be okay," said Mother. "Just don't tell anybody what's really inside. Oh, and here is a package of tissues for each of you. You can put them into your pocket," said Mother, handing over two small tissue packets to Taro and Hannah.

"Mom, what about the *hanka* and the *napukin*? We've *got* to have those today," said Hannah.

"I'm sorry, Hannah, they don't have them on Iwagi. I checked everywhere. I'll go to another island today. Don't worry. Just tell your teacher that your mother couldn't find any on the island and that you will bring them tomorrow," said Mother.

"Oh…." said Hannah in a worried voice.

Mother quickly jumped in. "But look, Hannah, our neighbour Furumura san found this lovely yellow hat for you. It used to be her granddaughter's hat when she went to Iwagi Shogakko."

"Oh, let's see …." said Hannah, forgetting about the *napukin* and the *hanka* and admiring her new yellow hat in the mirror.

Soon the small group of school children could be seen at the top of the lane. "Oh look, here they come, quick," said Mother, encouraging Taro and Hannah on with their packs and hurrying them out the door.

"*Ohayo gozaimasu*," sang out the small group of children.

"*Ohayo*," said Taro and Hannah in strong voices as they took up their positions at the back and waved goodbye.

Mother and Father sat down to breakfast. They washed down the large, thick slices of white toast with instant coffee.

"Go and have a look up the street to see what kind of garbage people are throwing out today," said Mother to Father. Mother never seemed to know what garbage went out on which days. It had been explained to her a number of times but she was still confused. Every second Tuesday cans were to be put out in the proper bins at the corner of their lane. On Thursdays it was *nama gomi*—raw garbage: food stuffs and vegetable peelings. Plastic bottles went out on Wednesdays. It was all a little overwhelming for Mother, who sensed that the neighbours were watching her closely to see if she was doing the right thing. And although most people were friendly enough, there brewed a certain suspicion of foreigners. Mother and Father and Taro and Hannah were already famous on the island. It seemed they were the only foreign family living on Iwagijima.

In the supermarket, Mother towered above the old ladies. They would sometimes glance into Mother's basket to see what she was buying, then whisper secretively to one another and smile. Mother would spend long minutes looking at the large and varied selection of fish and seafood. She wanted to buy something but had no idea how to prepare it. Inevitably, she chose meat or chicken.

If Mother was looking for something or if she was not sure about something she would usually ask the cashier or another shopper. Mother would assess the friendliness of their faces before asking for help. She knew that some people were nervous of foreigners and she didn't want to get caught in any embarrassing situations if she could help it.

Other times, when Mother did not want to risk creating a scene in the supermarket, she simply guessed. She would carefully study the shape and the contents of the product and decipher as much of the language as she was able and then she would boldly go through the cash stand. Most of the time she was right about what she thought the product was. A few times, she was wrong.

"Oooh yuck, what's this?" asked Hannah one day, as she bit into a bread roll that was stuffed with bean paste. Taro and Hannah didn't much like the sweet bean paste that the Japanese were so fond of. Another time, Taro remarked: "Mom, this isn't milk, it's liquid yogurt!"

Afterwards, Mother was sure to study the finer details of the carton so that she wouldn't make the same mistake twice. She also learned to be suspicious of bread items. She began to weigh the packages. The heavier ones, she guessed, would be filled with the dreaded bean paste. From then on, she always picked the lightest bag.

CHAPTER 7

KYUUSHOKU-LUNCHTIME AT IWAGI SHOGAKKO

"We're home!" shouted Taro and Hannah from the *genkan*.

"How was school?" asked Mother. "I bought *napukins* and *hankas* for you from Innoshima. And Hannah, I bought some buttons we can sew on to your jacket uniform."

"Naaaah, it's okay, Mom, I don't need buttons. Everyone's uniform jacket is missing buttons. Mine just looks normal the way it is. Can I see the *napukins*?"

Mother showed Hannah and Taro what she had bought.

"Oh, can I have this one. I like this one… this is perfect. Thanks, Mom." Hannah chose a blue *napukin* with flowers on it.

"How was school?" asked Mother again.

"It was good. Look, I got a present from Nene chan's grandmother. Can I open it?"

"Sure, go ahead," said Mother.

"Oh look, Mom, it's so pretty. Did she make these, do you think?" asked Hannah, holding out two small cloth dolls. "There's a letter too. Let's see….ummm…I think it says that I can go and play with Nene chan one day after school at her grandmother's. They have a dog and chickens and a pond with fish and turtles. Taro can come too."

"Oh boy," said Taro. "Can we go sometime Mom?"

"Well, I don't see why not, I think that would be fun," said Mother.

As Mother prepared an after school snack, Taro and Hannah chatted about their day at school.

"How was lunch?" asked Mother. "Did you get to wear your doctor's uniform, Hannah?"

"No, only the kids who are serving the food get to wear that. But Miyamoto sensei said that once I learn everything, I can have a turn too."

"That's great, Hannah," said Mother.

"Lunch was delicious," said Taro.

"No," said Hannah. "It was awful!"

"Well, I liked it," said Taro.

"Yaa, well, that's 'cause you like fish. I hate fish!" said Hannah.

"So … what was for lunch, Taro?" asked Mother.

"It was so good! We had this kind of soup with vegetables and a little salad and rice with fish."

"I only ate some of the rice," said Hannah, "the part that didn't have fish on it. Everything had fish in it. There were even these little tiny fishes in the salad, with heads on them. Yuck! Why do they have to put fish on everything?" complained Hannah.

"Mom, can we have Canadian food at home, since I have to eat Japanese food at school everyday?"

"Well, I've got an idea," said Mother. "How about we have a Canada Day every Friday and I'll make something Canadian for you for dinner," she said. "We'll celebrate the end of the week!"

"Yaa, that's a great idea!" said Hannah.

"Hurray, can we eat hamburgers and chips and coke?" asked Taro.

"We'll see," said Mother.

KYUUSHOKU-LUNCHTIME AT IWAGI SHOGAKKO

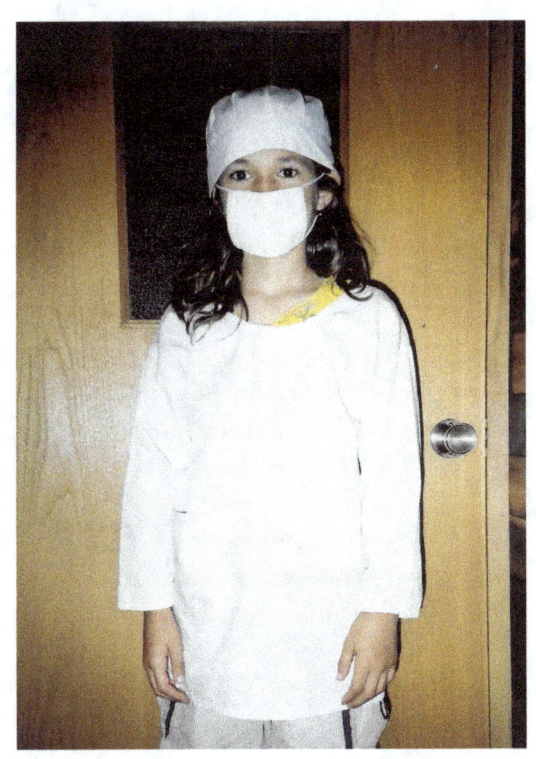

'Serving lunch uniform'
Dr. Frankenstein at Iwagi Shogakko

CHAPTER 8

FISHING IN IWAGIJIMA

Mother, Father, Taro and Hannah, got off of their bicycles to check out the catch of an *obaasan*—a grandmother, who was fishing along the sea wall. Her pail was teeming with small, sleek silver fish. Taro and Hannah could see her line in the clear water. The bait had been placed in a thumbsized metal basket which was attracting the fish to it. She tried to scare off the baby fugu fish which were eating her bait.

"Shoo, shoo," she hissed, as she gently shook her rod. "I don't want these fish biting my hooks," she said. "*Kore wa dame desu ne!*—Bad, very bad!"

"Dad," said Hannah, "Why doesn't she want to catch those fish?"

"Oh," said Father, "those fish are very poisonous. In English we call them puffer fish because they puff up their bodies like a balloon. The Japanese actually pay a lot of money to eat them at restaurants but they can only be prepared by specially trained chefs. They're really pretty neat looking fish, aren't they?"

"What happens if I touch one of those fish?' asked Hannah. "Will I die?"

"No, no, Hannah. It is only the inside of the fish, the liver, which is poisonous. Come on, let's go up near the port. I've seen people catching *iwashi-*sardines, up there."

When they arrived near the port, they put down their bicycles and began to prepare the rods. It was Father's job to prepare the lines and Mother's to fill the bait baskets with smelly shrimp mush. She used the flat side of a bamboo *yakitori* stick to poke the bait into the baskets.

"Is it ready, is it ready? Can I fish now?" asked Taro impatiently.

Father handed Taro and Hannah each a fishing rod. "Now, listen to me," he said. "Be sure to place the line and basket into the water very slowly." Before he had time to explain why, Taro had plunked his line in and upturned the bait basket. Fish started to swarm Taro's line, gobbling up the bait that was now floating about.

"Look, look at all the fish……but Dad….I don't have any bait left."

Father shrugged and smiled at Mother. He took Taro's line out once again and waited for Mother to refill the small metal basket with bait. He helped Taro to slowly lower the line into the water.

"Dad, Dad" yelled Hannah. "I've caught some fish. Look, look, help me!"

Father gently pulled out Hannah's line.

"Look, Taro, look…I've caught three *iwashis*," yelled Hannah, dancing excitedly around her fishing rod as Father unhooked the fish and slipped them into the bucket.

"Mom, look, I've caught three. They're swimming in my bucket. Taro, look!"

By this time, Taro's line had a swarm of fish around it. Father pulled it up to reveal another three hooked fish.

"Put them in here!" yelled Hannah rushing over with the bucket. Father slipped in Taro's three fish. Hannah watched the six silver fish swirling around in her bucket.

"I need more bait, Mom," called Taro.

"Me, too!" yelled Hannah

Mother quickly poked more mush into the baskets. "Put your lines back into the water," she said.

FISHING IN IWAGIJIMA

A middle-aged gentleman, amused by the curious sight of foreigners fishing, stopped by to have a look. He looked into the bucket and smiled. "They're good if you make them into tempura," he said.

"Yes, I'll have to try that," replied Mother.

"Oh, you speak Japanese very well, where are you from? Why are you here in Iwagi?" inquired the gentleman.

Mother explained that Taro and Hannah were going to school at Iwagi Shogakko.

He looked over at the children and then back at Mother. "She is your daughter?" he asked.

"Yes," said Mother. "And the boy is my son."

The man looked once again at the children and then back at Mother. "But, but …..he is Japanese. The boy is Japanese. He speaks English very well. How did he learn to speak English so well? It is strange. He is Japanese but he is speaking English," he exclaimed.

Mother could tell by his face that he was very confused at what he was seeing and hearing. Mother tried to explain.

"You see, Taro is adopted. We adopted him more than nine years ago while I was teaching at a university in Tokyo. But he has lived in Canada his whole life. I wanted him to learn about Japan."

The man had heard the words but judging from the expression on his face, he could simply not comprehend what he had just been told.

"*Ah, so desu ka*—I understand," he said politely. "But how can he speak English? He is Japanese."

Mother smiled. People on the island were more surprised that Taro could speak English than they were that she or Hannah could speak Japanese. Sometimes the islanders would stand at a distance and watch Taro and Hannah chatting away and playing in English. They looked on in disbelief as Taro spoke. It just didn't seem to make sense to them.

With the sun going down and a great bucket full of fish, it was time to head home. "How many do we have?" asked Father.

Hannah and Taro began counting : "One , two, three, four, five………thirty-eight. Wow, we have thirty eight fish!" The two children looked up at the Japanese gentleman who was still watching them with curiosity.

"*San ju happiki*—thirty eight fish!" said Hannah, proudly holding up the bucket for him to see.

"*Ehhh…….san ju happiki? Sugoi desu ne*—Incredible!" said the gentleman.

Father and Taro: Fishing for 'iwashi'—sardines

CHAPTER 9

CANADA DAY

Mother kicked down her kickstand and parked her bike beside the *takoyaki*—octopus ball stand, in front of the supermarket. The wafting smells of cooking *takoyaki* made her hungry and she hurried inside. It was cool, almost cold, inside. It was the only cool place Mother could find on the island. Sometimes, usually just before a typhoon the air became unbearably hot and so thick that she found it difficult to breathe. The air in the supermarket now felt fresh and she breathed it in deeply.

Mother circled the aisles slowly, scouring the shelves for things that she could use to make her 'Canada Day' dinner. It was Friday, and Mother wanted to keep her promise. She chose four narrow cans of coke, a package of hamburger, a tiny bottle of ketchup, some Japanese cheese, tomatoes and lettuce. She smiled when she found a very small packet of french fries in the freezer compartment. She looked at the price; 'Hmm… seven hundred yen, about eight or nine dollars.' She hesitated for a few seconds and then placed the french fries into her basket. 'There would be just enough for the children,' she thought. At the 'Baked Goods' section she surveyed the buns. All, it seemed, were heavy, most likely filled with the dreaded bean paste. Mother picked a standard loaf of thick white bread slices. 'I'll just have to cut the corners off,' she thought to herself and made her way to the cashier stand.

At home, Taro lay sprawled out on the tatami mat in front of the fan, playing Gameboy. "Hi Taro, where is everyone?" asked Mother.

"Oh, Dad and Hannah went down to the beach," replied Taro without looking up from his game. "And Ikeda san came by and dropped off a box of stuff. It's in the *genkan*."

Mother took a look inside the box. It was filled with vegetables from Ikeda san's *hatake*—field. There were a dozen or more cucumbers, some eggplants, squash and green beans. She bent down and opened the tiny refrigerator's door. It was as she expected, already jam packed with fruits and vegetables and Japanese pickles. All the neighbours were so kind, especially Mr. Ikeda and the Furumuras, who lived just a few doors down. Almost everyday someone would knock on the door. When Mother went to answer it, she would find that they had brought something: fruit and vegetables from their *hatake* or homemade dishes from their kitchen.

"You must put these in your refrigerator," Mrs. Furumura would say. "It is too hot to leave them out."

Mother would smile and say, "Yes, they had best be put in the refrigerator. They look delicious!" Then she, too, would smile and bow and head off back to her home.

❧

Everyone on Iwagi had a *hatake*. And since most of the islanders were retired, they had plenty of time to tend to their gardens. Fruits and vegetables grew in abundance in the island's hot, humid climate and very fertile soil. There was simply too much food produced for the islanders to eat and they didn't know what to do with it. It was not uncommon to see, off in a corner of the *hatake*, rotting piles of fruits and vegetables being composted for next year's crops.

CANADA DAY

"Wash up your hands," yelled Mother to Hannah as Hannah stepped into the *genkan*. "Dinner's almost ready."

"Oh boy, I'm starved," said Hannah. "What's for dinner anyway?"

"We're having hamburgers, chips and coke," replied Mother proudly.

"Taro, we're having hamburgers and coke!" yelled Hannah. "It's Canada Day, remember, Friday?"

"Coke? oh boy, coke!" exclaimed Taro. "Can I make a coke float?" asked Taro.

Taro, Hannah and Father sat down at the low table. Mother brought out each plate.

"What's this?" asked Hannah pointing to the bread with the corners cut off.

"What do you think it is?" replied Mother.

"The hamburger?" asked Hannah. "It looks funny."

"It looks delicious! Thanks, Mom," interjected Taro, as he bit down on the burger. "Mmmm, it's good!"

Hannah tentatively took a bite of hers. "Mmmm, you're right, Taro. It doesn't look like a hamburger but it tastes like one."

Mother went back into the kitchen and came out with a plate piled high with long peeled cucumbers. She placed it in the middle of the table. "Everyone is to eat at least four cucumbers," she said. "I need to make room in my fridge."

"I like Fridays," said Hannah, in between mouthfuls of her dinner. "We get Canada Day. We get the weekend. And at school on Fridays, we get 'Daybeedo sensei.'"

"Daybeedo sensei? Who is that?" asked Mother.

"Oh, 'Daybeedo sensei' is an Australian teacher. He comes to our school on Fridays to teach us English. I love English class," said Hannah.

"Me too," said Taro. "It's soooo easy!"

HANNAH CHAN

"I am the best in my class," said Hannah.
"Me too," said Taro.

CHAPTER 10

OFURO-THE BATH

"It's too hot, ouch, I can't get in!" called out Hannah from the *ofuro*.

Mother went over to the bath to see what the problem was. "You just need to add a little more cold water, that's all. And make sure you rinse off all of the soap before you get in."

"I know, I know…. what's the big deal anyway? In Canada we can wash *in* the bath. Why can't I do that here?" protested Hannah.

"Well, we're not *in* Canada and this is not a *Canadian* bath, is it?" said Mother.

"So….who cares….besides *I'm* not Japanese. I don't have to do it the Japanese way."

Mother knew that Hannah was tired and anxious and eager to pick a fight. Mother did not have the energy for argument. "Here, let me help you," she said in a soothing tone. She cooled the water in the bath and gently rinsed the soapy water from Hannah's hair. "Now, step into that….. and tell me how it feels."

Hannah slipped her body slowly into the bath. The warm water washed over her and enveloped her completely. Only her head poked out from the clouds of steam, which rose and swirled around her.

"Ahh…. that's perfect. Can you come in too?" she asked.

HANNAH CHAN

The Japanese *ofuro*—bath was different than the ones in Canada. Instead of being long and shallow it was small and deep. One was supposed to sit in the bath and have the warm water cover the shoulders. It was quite common for parents and young children to sit together in the bath. This was called *skinshippu* and it was a time for bonding and for relaxation. The Japanese loved their baths.

"Well, it's a little bit small Hannah, for both of us, but how about if I shower while you soak in the bath?"

Hannah wiped away a tear that had run down her cheek. "Thank you, Mommy. It's a little bit hard going to school in Japan," she said in a soft voice.

"I know, Hannah," said Mother. "It is hard, really hard! You are a brave little girl and remember, it's only for a short time. You are doing so well and I am very proud of you," said Mother.

"I love you, Mommy," said Hannah.

CHAPTER 11

LUNCH AT MACDONALD'S

After stopping at several islands to pick up other, mostly elderly passengers, the ferry sounded its horn at Innoshima, the final stop.

"Is this Fukuyama?" asked Hannah as she was getting off of the ferry boat.

Mother had promised Taro and Hannah a special lunch at MacDonald's restaurant. The only problem was that the nearest MacDonald's that she knew of was a very long way from Iwagijima. In fact, by boat and by bus it would take more than two hours to get there. Mother was not too worried about this. She thought that the outing itself would be fun for all of them. After all, there was an important castle to see in Fukuyama.

"No, I'm afraid we are still a long way from Fukuyama," said Mother. "We'll have to wait here for thirty minutes for the next connecting bus. I'd like both of you to go to the washroom." Taro wandered off to the mens' room on his own. "Hannah, you'd better go too," said Mother.

"I don't need to go," replied Hannah.

"It's a long way. I want you to go. I can't ask the bus driver to stop for you to go pee," said Mother. Hannah put down her Archie comic.

"Oh, alright," she said as she walked off in the direction of the ladies' toilet. After only a few seconds, she returned.

"You went already?" asked Mother. "That was fast."

"No, I couldn't," she said, with her arms folded defiantly in front of her. "It stinks bad in there and there's no Canadian toilet, only those squat kind!"

Mother sighed. "Hannah, shut your eyes," she said.

"What?" asked Hannah.

"Shut your eyes and open your hand."

Hannah shut her eyes and held out her upturned palm. Mother opened her purse, pulled out a hundred yen coin from her wallet and slipped it into Hannah's hand. Hannah opened her eyes and smiled. "Okay, okay, I'll try," she said and walked off once again towards the ladies' washroom.

૭૦૨૭

The bus to Fukuyama was better than the average Japanese commuter bus. It had places to store luggage. It had drink holders, and pockets to put books or magazines into. Taro and Hannah luxuriated in the large, clean, comfy seats. They adjusted their air flow vents so that cool air blew right into their faces. They put their canned soft drinks into the cup holders and then fiddled with the buttons and levers to get their seats to recline to an almost sleeping position.

"Mom, can you reach me my drink and Archie comic," asked Hannah, lounging back like a princess. Mother handed them over to her. "Hey, Taro, where did you get those?" asked Hannah, looking over at Taro's feet. Taro had removed his shoes and had pulled on a pair of adult sized slippers.

"They're right there, beside you," replied Taro pointing to the metal holder on the window side of the seat.

"Huh, they've got slippers?! Can I use them, Mom?" asked Hannah.

LUNCH AT MACDONALD'S

"Well, I guess that's what they're there for, go ahead," said Mother as Hannah kicked off her sandals.

✿

The bus wound its way along the shoreline of Innoshima and across several of the bridges that joined the string of islands together. Mother relaxed in the coolness and glanced absently out the window, nodding off from time to time. After about an hour, when the lush fields of tobacco turned first into dreary box-like apartments and then to gaudy, neon blinking megastores, Mother told Taro and Hannah to put on their shoes and gather up their things.

"Oh boy, are we almost there? I'm starving!" said Taro.

"Look, there's the MacDonald's right there, right beside the station," said Mother.

When the bus finally stopped, Taro and Hannah waited patiently for the other passengers to get off and then made their way up to the front of the bus.

"*Arigato,*" they said as they pushed their tickets into the slot and climbed down the bus stairs.

Taro and Hannah raced along the sidewalk and into the MacDonald's. Mother followed behind. They hadn't been to a MacDonald's restaurant in a very long time, not since they had left Canada. The idea of having real Canadian food was very exciting to them.

"Do you know what you want?" asked Mother.

"Yes, yes," they said as they stepped up to the counter.

"*Irrashaimase*—welcome," sang out the clerks behind the counter.

"I'll have the Big Mac Set," said Taro, pointing to the picture of the Big Mac Set on the plastic photo card that had been placed in front of him.

"Hmm, and I'll have the McKids Meal," said Hannah, "with a coke."

The clerk showed Hannah a selection of three toys to choose from. The toys were all very babyish, thought Hannah. "Mom, I don't want the toy—they're for babies," she said.

"Alright," said Mother. "She'll have the McKids Meal but we don't need the toy," she said to the young lady in Japanese.

"*Ehhhh*....which toy do you want?" asked the lady again.

"Oh, she doesn't want to have a toy. They are a little bit young for her," replied Mother.

The young clerk shifted restlessly on her feet and looking a bit flustered she said: "But you must have a toy, it comes with the meal."

Mother smiled politely. "Oh, but it's alright," she said. "We don't need one."

"*Sssaaa*… but if you don't want a toy you cannot order the McKids Meal set, you must order your meal *betsu, betsu*—separately."

"Oh, I see," said Mother. "Alright then, she will take a hamburger, a coke, and small fries. How much will that be?" she asked the clerk.

"Coke, hamburger, fries… that will be five hundred and twenty yen," said the clerk.

"Oh," said Mother a little confused. "But the McKids Meal is only three hundred and fifty yen for the same thing." Mother tried again. "I'll just take the McKids Meal but you can keep the toy."

The young lady became quite agitated now and looked helplessly to either side trying to get the attention of a colleague who could help her out with these *gaijin*—foreigners, but all of them were busy. "*Sumimasen*—I'm sorry," she said apologetically to the customers who were patiently waiting in line behind Mother and the children.

"I'm sorry. You can not order the McKids Meal without the toy," she said.

Mother, too, was beginning to get flustered. She sensed a lot of eyes on the back of her head. "Well then," she said. "I will have the McKids Meal with the toy please."

LUNCH AT MACDONALD'S

Once again the clerk placed the three toys in front of Hannah. "Which one do you like?" she asked.

Hannah, looking a little embarrassed said, "Mom, I don't really want *any* of them."

"Pick one!" said Mother curtly.

Hannah pointed her finger at the twirling Snoopy on wheels and moved to the side of the line.

CHAPTER 12

THE TELEPHONE

Mother dreaded the sound of the telephone ringing. She knew that neither Taro, nor Hannah, nor even Father, would go near it.

"Mom, telephone!" yelled Taro and Hannah together.

"Get it please!" Mother called back from the upstairs balcony where she was taking in the laundry. It kept right on ringing. No one would answer it. It was a lot of work answering the telephone, having to switch one's mind from English to Japanese. It caused Mother a lot of anxiety. What if she didn't understand what the other person was saying, or didn't know how to say the right thing in response?

Mother rushed down the stairs. There were very few people who called. Sometimes, Mother's friend Yoko, who lived in Nagoya, would call, or another of Mother's good friends, Machiko, would call from Tokyo. When she lifted the receiver and heard one of these voices, she would smile and relax. They both spoke English and a kind of Japanese that she could easily understand. But more often than not it would be either Mr. Ikeda or Mrs. Ikeda, from the island. Neither of them could speak English and Mother was not yet familiar with their dialect of Japanese. The words and phrases were different and the accent was different too. It was difficult to understand. It took

Mother's complete attention to understand even a little of what they were saying.

Mrs. Ikeda never phoned just to chat. Her phone calls were simply for relaying important official information regarding school forms, or electricity bills, or telephone lines and the like. At the same time, Mother was well aware that she was a lot of trouble for Mrs. Ikeda. In fact, without the help of Mr. and Mrs. Ikeda, Mother and the children would never have been able to come to Iwagijima at all. Mrs. Ikeda had been so kind to take on the huge responsibility of helping the family get settled on Iwagijima.

Poor Mrs. Ikeda, there was always much business to take care of and she didn't want Mother to make too many mistakes. Sometimes she would call on Mondays to remind Mother to put out her cans and bottles. Sometimes she would inform Mother that the gas man would be coming by to change the tanks and would need to be paid. It was no doubt a worry for Mrs. Ikeda to oversee a foreign family. Any problems arising from their stay on the island would immediately be reported back to her.

For example, there was the time the children were seen swimming at the beach before the official start of swimming season. This had created quite a commotion on the island. They had apparently been spotted by an islander who had been driving along the windy island road. Having witnessed such an unusual sight, he immediately reported what he saw, back to Mrs. Ikeda. Mrs. Ikeda, then, called Mother about the incident.

Mother especially dreaded picking up the telephone and hearing Mrs. Ikeda's voice. Mother was always on edge in case she or the children had done something wrong. Perhaps she had included the wrong type of garbage for Thursday's garbage removal. Or maybe

THE TELEPHONE

she had forgotten to pay the bill for the newspaper. Some mistakes, however, Mother could never fully comprehend.

The ban on swimming, was something that Mother did not really understand. It was hot, very hot. The beaches were sandy and the waters were clear and refreshing. What harm could come of swimming before the official date? Besides, it was next to impossible to tell Taro and Hannah that they were not allowed to go into the water. Mother had half-heartedly tried to stop them one day, but when they retorted, 'Why not! It's way hotter here than in Canada,' she had felt at a bit of a loss as to what to say. When she had explained about the official date, the children just looked up at her. 'Huh?' they had said, as if she were crazy.

Soon Mother gave up and let them go in. She tried to find remote areas where no one would be watching. And she let them swim in their clothes, thinking that if someone did in fact catch them swimming it would not look as though it had been planned.

༄ༀ༄

Mother reached over and picked up the telephone. *"Moshi moshi—* hello," she said. Thank goodness, she thought to herself, when she heard the voice on the other end. The call was not from Mrs. Ikeda. It was from Mr. Ikeda.

Mr. Ikeda was not at all officious. He did not seem to worry about the family making mistakes or forgetting to pay their bills. He didn't mind if Mother or the children made mistakes in Japanese. It didn't seem to bother him either if no one could understand what he was saying on the phone. He just seemed to like to talk or to come over to visit. He truly loved to teach Mother, Father and the children about Iwagi. Iwagi was his island. It was a beautiful island and he was very proud of it. There were so many exciting experiences to share with this Canadian family.

After focusing hard and trying to chat for a few minutes, Mother put down the receiver.

"Who was that?" asked Hannah

"It was Ikeda san," replied Mother.

"Uh, oh," said Taro. "What do we have to do now?" he asked.

"I'm not sure," replied Mother.

"What do you mean?" asked Taro suspiciously. Taro knew that a call from Ikeda san usually meant an outing of some sort, often very early on a weekend morning, the *only* 'sleep in' mornings. "I'm *not* getting up early tomorrow Mom … please!"

"Well, I couldn't quite understand everything but I think it's tonight he's talking about," said Mother.

"Tonight!" yelled Taro and Hannah together.

"What are we going to do tonight?" asked Hannah.

"Well, I might be wrong, but I think Mr. Ikeda is taking you bug hunting.

Swimming before the official start of swimming season

CHAPTER 13

BUGS AT NIGHT

"*Kiotsukete*!—be careful!" yelled Mother from the doorway. Taro and Hannah and Father followed Ikeda san down the dark, narrow lane. They weren't really sure where they were going or what exactly they were about to do.

"I wish Mom had come with us," whispered Hannah to Father. Hannah knew that without Mother around, the pressure to make conversation or to answer questions would be on her or Taro. Father was pretty much useless. He would just smile and make sounds like *mmm* or *hai*, but really he wouldn't know much about what was going on.

At the end of the lane, Ikeda san smiled and motioned for them to get into his truck. There was only enough room for Mr. Ikeda and Father to sit comfortably in the tiny truck's cab.

"We can't *all* fit in here, can we?" said Taro.

"Hannah, you climb up here on my lap," said Father.

"But Dad, where am *I* going to sit. There's no space left," said Taro.

Father pressed his knees over to one side. Hannah bumped her head on the cab's roof. "Youch," she cried. "Crouch down on the floor," said Father. Taro climbed in, jostled to secure a foothold and balanced his body by holding on to Father's legs. Father slowly squeezed the door until he could hear a click. Ikeda san switched on the ignition and they were off.

After a few minutes they turned off the main island road and onto a very steep, narrow dirt and gravel path. The night was dark. The road was bumpy. It was a little bit scary. Ikeda san swerved to avoid potholes and the rickety truck lurched and jangled its way up the hill. No one spoke. Near the top, Ikeda san turned off his engine and got out. He carried an extendable pole, a flashlight and an empty yogurt container. Father, Hannah and Taro followed.

The darkness was thick and hot and filled with sounds. The chirping and clicking and whirring surrounded them.

"What are we going to do now, Dad?" asked Hannah in a quiet voice, a little unsure of the adventure about to unfold. She did know, however, that she was darn happy that Mother had made her wear long pants and running shoes instead of the shorts and sandals that she had insisted on wearing. "Why do I have to wear long pants? It's hot out there!" she had complained to Mother. Now, with the sounds of the jungle crawling all around her, Hannah was happy to have her feet and legs safely covered.

"This is cool!" said Taro as Ikeda san moved the beam of light from the flashlight into the trees and bushes while walking along. Mr. Ikeda stopped in front of a tree and traced the beam of light slowly up the trunk. He pointed upwards. Father, Taro and Hannah gathered around.

"H..o..l..y..!" exclaimed Hannah. "Look Dad, up there!" The tree trunk was alive and crawling with bugs and insects.

"Look... *Kuwagata*," exclaimed Taro, pointing up the tree. "Those are *Kuwagata* beetles," he announced. "They eat the sap."

Taro and Hannah had learned at school that the best beetles to catch were the fighting beetles: the *kuwagata* and the *kabutomushi*. They looked like armoured tanks with their hard black shells and

BUGS AT NIGHT

menacing horns. "Dad, these cost a lot of money in Tokyo," said Taro. "The kids at school told me that the really special big ones can cost about a million yen each!"

"Wow, a million yen!" said Hannah. "How much is that Dad, in Canadian dollars? Maybe we can catch a whole bunch and sell them!"

Mr. Ikeda extended his pole. Reaching up the trunk, he snagged the beetles in his net. He lowered the pole and transferred the beetles from the net to the yogurt container. He passed the container to Hannah and continued along the path, shining his light on the trees and bushes as he moved along. When he spotted *kuwagata* or *kabutomushi* he would raise his net, catch as many as he could and put them into Hannah's container. After about twenty minutes the yogurt container was crawling with beetles.

Suddenly, Taro screamed, "AHHHH!" and jumped to the other side of the path. Hannah tightened her grip on Father's hand.

"What, Taro. What's wrong?" she yelled, afraid to move an inch.

"There's a humungous spider!" Taro yelled back to Hannah. "I hate spiders!"

Just then, Ikeda san, who had climbed up onto a nearby ledge, lost his footing and tumbled to the ground, losing his pole and his glasses on his way down. Hannah and Taro screamed and Father rushed towards him.

"*Daijoubu*—Are you okay?" he asked.

"*Daijoubu, daijoubu*—okay, okay," replied Mr. Ikeda.

He had come just inches from falling into a swamp. Father spotted his glasses and retrieved them with one hand while steadying Mr. Ikeda with the other.

"I want to go home," whispered Hannah to Father.

"Me too," said Taro.

Ikeda san got himself up and brushed off his clothing. With an embarrassed smile he looked over at Taro and Hannah. "*Kaeroka*—shall we go back?" he asked.

"*Unh*—yes!" said the children together.

On the ride home, Hannah clutched the yogurt container tightly in one hand. With the other hand she held a small stick. When the beetles crawled up the sides to the top and threatened to escape, she gave them a poke with her stick. She looked over at Mr. Ikeda. "*Tanoshikatta*—that was fun!" she said.

CHAPTER 14

CRABS

By the third week, Taro and Hannah had settled in quite nicely to the daily routines and schedules of Iwagi Shogakko. The uniforms and school supplies had sorted themselves out. They seemed to know when to wear what shoes and how to do most of their class work. Hannah had even discovered something at school that had made her quite happy: a western style toilet!

"I don't mind waiting for it, Mom, if it's busy. It's better than using those other kind," she said to Mother one day.

It was fun, Hannah thought, going to school without parents always being there. In Canada, kids usually got driven to school in the morning and then picked up from school in the afternoon. There was never any time to dilly or dally. But here on Iwagi, Hannah and Taro got to do whatever they wanted. They could choose any number of paths to get home. In the beginning they would get lost, but after a short time they became experts in finding their way around the small island.

Sometimes they would stop to catch bugs. Hannah's favourites were the stick bugs and the bright green praying mantises. Other days, they would head along the sea wall to see if anyone was fishing. If it was really, really hot, they might even take a detour up to one of the temples at the top of a hill. It would feel cooler up there. In the shade of the bamboo forests the swishing of the delicate branches made it feel like there was a breeze. They would dip their hands into the clear waters of the koi ponds when no one was looking or play hide and seek in amongst the stone statues.

If Mother was pleased with something they had done, she might give each of them one or two hundred yen coins in the morning, as they headed out the door, to spend on their way home from school. On those days, deciding what to buy was sometimes difficult; a cold drink from the vending machines, an ice cream from the supermarket, or a small toy from the trinket machines which were lined up outside of the small shops.

School was mostly fun too. It was a lot different than in Canada. Hannah liked that!

"Go outside, across to the beach, and collect as many different species of crab as you can find," directed Miyamoto sensei one afternoon. Hannah and the others in her group burst out the door with their containers in hand, across to the sandy beach. The afternoon would be spent chasing the scurrying creatures up and down the sand.

"*Atta!*—I've got one," shouted Toru chan as he scooped up a medium sized gray crab into his plastic container.

Hannah and Moegi chan were hunting down a larger, darker gray crab with a red star on its back at the other end of the beach. "Hannah chan *hayai deshoo*—you are fast. You trap it under your container and I'll push it in with my stick."

"*Iii yo*—okay, I'll try," said Hannah. Hannah waited for the crab to emerge from its hole and pounced after it. "*Yatta*—I did it," she yelled as she plunked the container down on top of the speeding crab. Moegi chan rushed over to help. Hannah carefully lifted up the rim of the container. "Eeeyaaa!" they screamed, as the crab darted away and down into a nearby hole. Moegi chan dug furiously with her stick but it was no use. The crab was much too fast. "*Are*—darn it!" she exclaimed under her breath.

Miyamoto sensei, meanwhile, wandered from one group to the other group to see how they were doing. "Oh my goodness," he teased the children. "The bug catching group over in the field is doing much better than you are. They have many, many more bugs than you have crabs."

"How many do they have?" challenged Sayaka kun.

"We can get twice as many as they can!" yelled Jun chan.

Miyamoto sensei smiled and with his hands clasped behind his back, he meandered off along the beach.

Hannah liked Miyamoto sensei. He often joked around with the children. He was fun and a little bit silly too. "Mom, you know what Miyamoto sensei did today?" Hannah asked Mother one day.

"No, what did he do?" asked Mother.

"Well, he was dancing and singing in class during math test," said Hannah.

"Oh, that's kind of strange, isn't it?" asked Mother.

"Yaa, I know…but he always does stuff like that. He makes us laugh a lot. And, oh brother, Mom, he always tries to speak English to me in class," exclaimed Hannah.

"Well, what's wrong with that?" asked Mother. "He's just trying to help you, isn't he?"

"Yaa, I guess so, but sometimes I get kind of embarrassed. Whenever he does that, all the kids look at me and I feel kind of stupid. His English is kind of weird and anyways, I already know what's going on. He doesn't have to tell it to me in English."

"Oh, he's probably just having some fun. You know, in Japan, everyone has to study English but they don't get much of a chance to use it," said Mother.

"Oh well, I don't care," said Hannah. "I like him. We get to do fun things in our class."

Miyamoto sensei blew his whistle, signaling all the children to come back into the classroom. Once everyone had settled back into their seats and had taken long swigs of cool tea from their thermos bottles, he explained what they were to do with their 'catches.'

"First," he said, "I want you to pick one of the more interesting bugs or crabs and draw it in your notebooks. Then, I want you to measure what you have caught. How long is it? How wide is it? How many centimeters is the biggest? How many centimeters is the smallest? Can you find any geometric shapes or interesting patterns?" he continued. The children listened attentively. Every now and then, they glanced down, making sure their 'catch' was not about to escape.

"Now begin," said Miyamoto sensei.

CRABS

Playing at the temples

Playing in the bamboo forest

Ringing the temple bells

CHAPTER 15

CLEANERS

After dinner, Mother cleared away the dishes and wiped down the low table with a damp cloth. "Where's your brother, Hannah?" she asked. "It's time for you two to start your homework."

"He's in the bathroom!" complained Hannah. "He's been in there forever! Taro, get out!" she yelled. "It's my turn to use it."

"Okay, okay, I'll be out in a minute," Taro yelled back.

Mother walked over to the bathroom door. She could hear the rapid clicking of buttons and the electronic music coming from his GameBoy. "Taro, it's time to start your homework," she called.

"Alright, alright," he said. "Just let me find a saving spot."

Taro spent a lot of time in the toilet. In fact, the toilet was a very popular room in the house. It was not much bigger than a broom closet in Canada, but it was the only room with a 'real seat' in it, even if that seat had a hole. Because of its back rest it was undoubtedly the most comfortable place for reading or for playing GameBoy, and it was often a source of competition and conflict.

The toilet was of a Western design but it did not flush. If Hannah lifted the cover, she could look a long, long way down the hole. In fact, it was difficult to make out where the hole actually ended. Hannah couldn't really see anything below in the darkness.

"Mom, where does it all go?" she asked one day.

"I guess it goes into a big holding tank," replied Mother. Mother too, was surprised by the toilet. This was the first toilet that she had seen in Japan that didn't flush. She was perhaps most surprised though, by the fact that it didn't really smell. There was no odour at all.

The odour came later, about two months after they had moved in. There was a knock on the door one morning after the children had gone to school. Mother opened the door to find two very rough looking characters, one male, one female, standing before her. They were shabbily dressed and had cigarettes dangling from their lips. They spoke to Mother in gruff voices, much too quickly for Mother to be able to understand. Their Japanese was different. The words and accents were unfamiliar to her. *"Sumimasen, wakarimasen*—I'm sorry, I don't understand," said Mother, but the two became agitated and spoke louder and faster, repeating the whole thing over again. Mother too, was getting flustered, because she didn't know why they were at her door. Mrs. Ikeda had not forewarned her about this visit. The only thing she did know was that the air outside was filled with the most putrid stench.

She looked up the lane and saw a small industrial truck with a hose on it. Suddenly, she understood. These two had come to empty her toilet tank. "*Ah, wakatta, wakatta,*—now I understand!" she said. The man and the woman smiled for the first time. Their harshness melted away. They had probably never before encountered a foreigner in their line of work and had been as afraid of Mother as Mother had been of them.

CHAPTER 16

A SURPRISE FOR TARO AND HANNAH

"How's your homework coming along?" asked Mother.
"I'm done!" said Taro.
"I only have two more questions," said Hannah.
Just then, there was a knock at the door. It was after eight o'clock. 'Hmm, I wonder who that is,' thought Mother. "I'll bet it's Mr. Ikeda," she said as she moved towards the *genkan*. She opened the door and sure enough Ikeda san was standing before her, clutching a box of vegetables fresh from his *hatake*.

"*Dozo*—please," he said, handing Mother the box. Inside, there were eggplants, asparagus, cobs of corn and a pumpkin.

"*Waa, oishi so*—these look delicious, *arigato*."

"Ah, the asparagus is not so good this year. There are only a few small ones. By the way, how are your onions? Do you need any more onions?" Ikeda san stepped into the kitchen and peered through the sliding glass doors of the tatami room to the outside platform. He quickly noticed the giant cardboard box overflowing with onions. "*Ah, mata aru ne*—you still have some I see," he said with a chuckle.

Ikeda san moved back out towards the entrance door. "I have brought something for the children," he said. "Taro kun, Hannah chan, *kite*—come!"

Hannah and Taro looked up. "*Nani*—what did you bring?" They followed him out to his small truck. He motioned for them to look into the back.

"*Are, nani*—what is that?" asked Taro, pointing to two large buckets.

Ikeda san reached over and pulled down one of the buckets.

"Turtles… look Mom, turtles!" exclaimed Hannah.

"Wow, look at that one… it's huge!" said Taro.

Ikeda san beamed in delight as the wide-eyed children peered excitedly into the bucket. He reached across and pulled over the second bucket.

"*Sugoi, mite*—wow, look!" said Taro.

The buckets contained about ten or more turtles. Some were small, about the size of a yoyo. Others were almost as big as a frisbee.

"What will we do with them, Mom?" asked Taro.

Mother looked over at Mr. Ikeda. She wasn't quite sure what she was to do with the turtles. Ikeda san looked at his watch.

"I've got to get going," he said. "Pick out which ones you want to keep and I'll come by tomorrow evening to collect the ones you don't need. I'll just throw them back into the pond."

"*Arigato*," said Mother and the children together.

"*Ii ee*—don't mention it," responded Mr. Ikeda as he stepped into the driver's seat and started his engine.

It was now well past nine o'clock.

"Mom, I want this cute little guy and that one there," said Hannah, pointing into the first bucket. "I get to have my own pet turtles," she said, smiling up at Mother. I'm going to have to write a letter and tell my friends in Canada. What do they eat Mom?" asked Hannah."

A SURPRISE FOR TARO AND HANNAH

Mother looked bewildered. "I don't know," she said. "But it *is* time for you to get ready for bed. Go wash up your hands and face and brush your teeth."

Taro put down his GameBoy. "Oh man, Mom, what's that smell?!" he said. "That's awful!"

☙❧

After the children had gone to bed, Mother made herself a cup of tea and sat down at the low table. She wondered what to do with the turtles. For the moment they were okay, in the *genkan*, crawling, one on top of the other, in their buckets. Taro was right! They smelled really bad! In the heat and humidity of the night, the smell of the muddy swamp turtles was overpowering, almost gagging. Mother thought of putting them out the door for the night. But she couldn't do that. Not with ten or more cats next door. She thought of putting them outside on the upper floor verandah where she hung out her laundry. But no… the sounds of their crawling would drive her crazy and prevent her from sleeping. Finally, she decided to close them up in the *ofuro*—bath. The doors would contain the foul odours a little and they would be far enough away from where she was sleeping. Mother was tired. She felt a little lonely and wished that Father was with her. But he was still away in Canada.

When Mother finally got up to bed, she found that the children were still awake. They lay together quietly in the hot, steamy night.

"Won't Daddy be surprised when he comes back from Canada?" whispered Hannah, "and sees all of our turtles!"

"Yes, I'm sure he will be," Mother whispered back. "Now shhhh, let's listen to all the sounds we can hear."

There were no car sounds, only the buzzing, the croaking, the whirring sounds of the forest and jungle. It was loud but somehow soothing in the darkness. It enveloped them completely.

HANNAH CHAN

"Mommy," whispered Hannah.
"Yes, Hannah."
"The hills are singing."

CHAPTER 17

SCHOOL DAYS

When Hannah got to class that morning the children were racing around the desks, laughing and squealing in delight.

"Catch them," yelled Shota kun as Take chan and Kenta kun chased after the creatures scurrying about on the floor. The boys had let out all of the crabs and were now madly trying to get them back into their containers before Miyamoto sensei arrived in the class room. Hannah joined in the fun.

'What an exciting way to start the day,' she thought to herself. The boys at Iwagi Shogakko were always full of mischief. At first, Hannah thought that because all the children wore uniforms, that somehow they would be much better behaved than the children in her class in Canada. But no… she soon learned that that was not so. The boys were even noisier and more troublesome than the boys back at home.

Hannah found one boy, in particular, to be very, very annoying. His name was Sayaka kun. He always wanted to sit right beside Hannah chan. At first, Hannah thought he was kind and helpful but after a while she grew very frustrated with him. "Mom, he just won't leave me alone," she said to Mother one evening. "He always wants to be in the group I'm in. He always wants to stand beside me. I don't know what to do. Every time I write a sentence, or put an answer in my notebook, or figure out a math problem, he is always there. He watches everything I do! He grabs my book or my paper and he says: 'No Hannah, that's wrong. You have to do it like this!' Then he crosses out my work and redoes it for me. Sometimes he calls out to Miyamoto sensei. '*Sensei, sensei,*' he says. 'Hannah made a mistake.' I feel so embarrassed! All the kids come rushing over to my desk to check what I have done. I just feel like crying! I hate him!"

"Hannah, Hannah, he is probably just trying to help you. I don't think he is trying to be mean. Sometimes, you know, when a boy is really annoying, it just means that he likes you," said Mother.

"MOM! EEYUUU!" retorted Hannah.

～～

The classroom door opened and Miyamoto sensei stepped inside. The children all stood up beside their desks. "*Ohayo gozaimasu!*" they called out to their teacher. "*Ohayo gozaimasu,*" replied Miyamoto sensei, and the children sat down in their seats to begin their day. The giggles had subsided. The crabs were safely back in their containers lined up along the windowsill of the classroom.

～～

There were so many things that were different about Iwagi Shogakko compared to school in Canada. One thing that really surprised Hannah was that the kids got to be in charge a lot of the time. For example, the kids were in charge of morning announcements over the public address system. The announcements were more interesting than the school announcements back home. Some days the kids in charge would broadcast a riddle or give a quiz. One morning, as Hannah was sitting at her desk listening, she heard her name being announced.

SCHOOL DAYS

She focused hard. It was kind of funny. She and Taro were part of the morning quiz. "Which part of Canada do Taro kun and Hannah chan come from," asked the announcing child. Hannah smiled. Some children in Hannah's class were quick to yell out the answer.

"*Bankooba*!" they yelled. That was how they said Vancouver in Japanese. Everyone in the whole school, and not just in Taro's and Hannah's own classes, knew everything about them. In fact, they were famous, not only at school but all across the island of Iwagi. Even though Hannah and Taro might not remember the names or faces of some of the kids outside of the school, the other children would be sure to recognize them. Little children from kindergarten class or big kids in sixth grade, knew who Taro and Hannah were. Sometimes, as they were walking along the street they would hear an *obaasan*—a grandmother, say to a small child: "Look, there's Taro kun and Hannah chan."

Sometimes after school Hannah would try to find an unpopular route home. She would purposely choose the lanes and alleys that would not be used by the main groups of school children.

Every now and then, if Hannah was very late, Mother would go off on her bicycle to look for her. She would come back home hot and frustrated at having been unable to locate her. "Where were you?" asked Mother to Hannah one day when she suddenly appeared in the doorway. "I've looked everywhere. Where were you?"

"I took a different way. A way where there aren't so many kids."

"Oh?" said Mother, a little bit surprised by the answer. "Why did you do that? Did you have some problems with the kids at school today?" she asked

"No Mom," said Hannah. "That's not why. You see, well, by the end of the day, I'm so tired of thinking and talking in Japanese that I just kind of need a break. It's not that I don't want to play with the others. It's just that, uh…"

Mother interrupted. " I understand. You just need some time to yourself, to relax, and not to have to worry about anything at all. I understand, Hannah." Mother put her arm around Hannah's shoulders and gave her a squeeze. "I need that too sometimes."

CHAPTER 18

COMPUTER CLASS

"Computer class is great!" announced Hannah to Mother one day. "I am one of the best in my class!"

"Oh," said Mother. "Is it a lot different than it is in Canada?" she asked.

"Well, a little," said Hannah. "We're learning how to type *romaji*—roman style letters. You know Mom, the letters in Japanese that go: *ra, ri, ru, re, ro*."

"Oh, I see," said Mother.

"And I can find the letters on the keyboard really fast, faster than everybody else."

Hannah felt very happy and pleased with herself when she was able to do things at school as well as, or even better than, the other kids. Most of the time, Hannah had to struggle to keep up, especially in 'Japanese Reading and Writing.' In Computer class or English class she never had to worry about Sayaka kun or Moegi chan, who was a little bit bossy, telling her how to do it, or tattling on her to the teacher for making a mistake. In English class everyone wanted to be on *her* team if they were playing a game. And in Computer class they fought to sit beside her. Hannah liked that. It made her feel proud.

"Alright everyone, please listen," called out Miyamoto sensei. "Stop typing and look at me. Jun chan, keep your feet to yourself, please!" he yelled over to two boys who were kicking each other under the table. The children stopped what they were doing and looked up at their teacher.

"You are all going to go outside and find the sounds that you have been typing," said Miyamoto sensei.

The children looked up at their teacher. "*Eh*…what do you mean?" they asked with confused expressions upon their faces. "What are we going to do?"

Miyamoto sensei waited until all the children were quiet and listening attentively. "I want you to go outside and listen to sounds, as many sounds as you can hear. Listen to the waves at the beach. Listen to the workmen's hammers. Listen to the leaves blowing or the babies crying at the nursery." Miyamoto sensei paused, then reduced his voice to a whisper. "Listen carefully, and try to write down in *romaji* the sounds that you can hear. Now off you go!

And off they went, pen and paper in hand to the world outside their classroom. In pairs and small groups they spread out in all directions. Some children could be seen listening to water pipes at the back of the school. Others stalked the tall dry grasses listening for bug sounds. Hannah thought that this was great fun. She had never before listened for sounds, 'in a Japanese way.' Sounds like; *ki, ki, ki*, or *muzu, muzu, muzu*, or *jidi, jidi, jidi* were new for her. No one wrote down Canadian sounds like 'drip' or 'ding' or 'crash' or 'splash.' It was all different, and it was fun.

CHAPTER 19

LEMONADE AND WHEELCHAIRS

"Mom, I'm home," yelled Hannah as she plunked down her school pack in the *genkan*. "Where are you? Mom!"

"I'm up here, Hannah. I'm just taking in the laundry," yelled Mother from the upstairs verandah.

"I brought you something. I want to show it to you," said Hannah in an urgent voice.

Mother put down the pail of clothes pegs and started down the stairs.

"Look Mom, these are for your tea," said Hannah, as she held out a palm full of shiny green leaves for Mother to see.

Mother took the leaves into her hand.

"Smell them," said Hannah, "but crush them up a little bit first. They smell way better that way."

Mother crushed the leaves and raised her hand to her nose. "Mmm, these *do* smell beautiful. What are they? They smell a little like lemons."

"That's right! They are from the 'lemon *hatake*'. We went up there today. You're supposed to put them into your tea. Why don't you try it, Mom," said Hannah.

"Well, alright. I *could* use a cup of tea right now," said Mother. Mother put the water on to boil and went to sit down in the tatami room. "So, when did you go to the lemon *hatake*?" asked Mother.

"Oh, Mom, it was so fun. We were sitting there, doing our work at our seats after lunch and then Miyamoto sensei said, 'Everyone shut your books and put your pencils away. We are going to the lemon *hatake*.'

I wasn't sure what he meant, but all the kids got so excited, and we got on our outdoor shoes and went outside. Miyamoto sensei has this *huge* black car. Everyone just piled in. Some squished into the front seat, some went into the back. I got to sit on the floor with Nami chan and Kana chan. No seatbelts or anything! It was *so* cool. Our whole class, in his car! Miyamoto sensei drove part way around the island and then he went up this bumpy path to the lemon *hatake*. We were all banging into each other and the boys were so loud that I had to cover my ears! They're *so* annoying!"

Mother poured the boiling water from the kettle over her teabag and the crushed lemon leaves. "What did you do at the *hatake*?" she asked.

"Well, we talked to the farmer and everyone asked him questions about growing lemons. He showed us lots of stuff, and then we all got to pick lemons. When we got back to school we made lemonade."

"Lemonade, oh, I'll bet that tasted pretty good. Fresh lemonade from lemons you picked yourself," said Mother.

"Un uh, well, not exactly. Miyamoto sensei couldn't find any sugar!"

Mother removed her tea bag and fished out the lemon leaves from her cup. She breathed in the fragrant rising steam before taking a sip of the tea. "Mmm, this *is* good," she said.

The one thing that Hannah really liked about going to school at Iwagi Shogakko was that a lot of their school work was done outside of the classroom. One class that the children had every day was called

LEMONADE AND WHEELCHAIRS

Iwagi benkyo—the study of Iwagi Island. In this class, the children got to go out into the community and learn about all sorts of things. They talked to the farmers and the fisherman and the boat builders. They talked to the manager of the Co-op supermarket. Usually, they would have to prepare questions to ask the 'experts,' and then later report back to the class on what they had learned.

✦

One day Hannah had come racing back from school and was very excited. "Mom, guess what we got to do today?" she asked Mother as she stepped into the *genkan* and unloaded her pack.

"I don't know. What did you get to do?" responded Mother, her curiosity piqued by Hannah's excitement.

"Well, we got to do exercises in wheelchairs!" exclaimed Hannah.

"Exercises in wheelchairs! What do you mean?" asked Mother

"Well, today for *Iwagi benkyo* my group got to walk to the *Fukushi Centa* near the port."

"What is the *Fukushi Centa*?" asked Mother.

"Well, it's kind of like this place where there's lots of old people," explained Hannah. "We got to have a tour and then we had to ask them lots of questions for our poster."

"Your poster?" questioned Mother.

"Yaa, we have to learn a bunch of things, then later, we make a poster and show it to the rest of the kids in our class," explained Hannah.

"Oh, I see," said Mother.

"It was so cool, Mom. We went to this kind of exercise room with all sorts of neat stuff in it, like big balls and mats and bars and rings hanging from the ceiling. I got to get in a wheelchair and pull myself up a kind of hill and then swing from the bars and ropes. It was really fun!"

"Wow, you're pretty lucky, Hannah. You don't get to do such fun things in Canada, do you?" said Mother, who always liked to play up the positive things that were happening to Hannah in Iwagi.

"No," said Hannah, "not usually. And the old people were so nice. They kept smiling at us and laughing. They were so happy to have us there. I think they really like seeing kids, Mom. Before we went back to school we sat down at these little tables with them, and had *ocha and o sembei*—green tea and rice crackers. I didn't really like the tea much, but the *sembei* were sure good. At my table, one old, old lady kept reaching over to touch my hand but you know what, Mom?"

"No, what Hannah?" asked Mother.

"I wasn't even afraid!"

CHAPTER 20

VERY OLD PEOPLE

Iwagi was not only an old island. It was an old island that was filled with very old people. Mother had never seen so many elderly all in one place before. She knew from reading the *Japan Times*, that Japan had one of the biggest and fastest growing aging populations in the world. In the bustle of Tokyo or Osaka one never noticed anything out of the ordinary. There were a few elderly folk on the trains and in the shops. In fact, it was very similar to Vancouver. But here on Iwagi, things looked different.

༺༻

"Mom," whispered Hannah one day, tugging on Mother's shirt, "Why is everyone pushing around those chairs, you know, with wheels on them. What are they for?"

"Those chairs, Hannah, are to help the old people to walk. When they get tired they can just sit down. Under the seat they can store things, like groceries or their purse. It's a pretty good idea, don't you think?"

"I, guess so," responded Hannah.

Sometimes, Mother would have to get after the children for pointing.

"Oh my God. Psst, Hannah, Mom, over there, see?" said Taro pointing across the street. "Whoa, how can she see?"

"Where's she going?" asked Hannah. "She's completely bent in half."

Although it was impolite to stare, Mother knew that Taro and Hannah had never seen anything quite like this before.

Hannah, who was small for her age, often stood taller than the elderly Japanese women. And there were a lot of elderly women. In fact, probably about seventy percent of the really old folk on Iwagi were women. They tended their gardens and the graves of their ancestors. They fished and chatted and took care of great grandchildren. The supermarket just before noon became a hubbub of activity. And the small clinic around the corner from the supermarket became a gathering place to exchange news and gossip and to gain sympathy for minor maladies. For the most part their lives looked pretty good.

Mother noticed, though, that sometimes life was tough for them. Many didn't seem to have anyone to care for them. Sons and daughters had long left Iwagi to pursue education and careers off of the tiny island. Once they left, they rarely returned.

Japanese live for a long time. More than once or twice Mother and the children would see what looked like an eighty year old slowly pushing a one hundred year old, in a wheelchair through the narrow streets and alleys. Though the scene was comical, it was not that unusual. Old, old ladies would be pushing their even older husbands up to the ferry terminus and onto the small ferry boats. They struggled to lift the wheelchairs up the ramps and over the ridges. There were no serious medical facilities on the island. Anything beyond the most minor of ailments had to be taken care of in hospitals further afield. When someone got stuck or was having difficulty maneuvering their wheelchair, Mother would rush towards them and make an awkward attempt to help. And though they were most likely grateful

VERY OLD PEOPLE

for the assistance, they seemed embarrassed, almost humiliated, by the attention.

The elderly really loved the children of Iwagi. Big fusses were made over the new babies and the toddlers on the island. There were only a few of them and they were celebrities. In the supermarket the young children were the kings and queens. The elderly customers would dig deep into their pockets and with a sparkle in their eye draw out candies and sweets to give to them. Even the check out ladies had a cache of treats hidden behind the counter.

At Iwagi Shogakko, Taro's and Hannah's school, enrollment was dwindling year by year. In the Grade One class there were just eight students, seven boys and one girl. In Mr. Ikeda's class a couple of generations earlier there had been more than fifty children in each classroom. The classrooms were large. But nowadays the few desks lined up at the front of the class seemed to get swallowed up by the expanse of emptiness.

In spite of this the school remained a cheerful and noisy place, even after school and on weekends. Iwagi Shogakko was not just a place for the children of Iwagi, it was also a center of the community. Grandparents would be paired up with the primary students for bowling, or would be asked to teach the children a traditional craft or dance. Parents might join their children for a game of dodgeball. In the large gymnasium and assembly hall there would be festivals and plays and magic shows and music performances. Everyone would be invited.

For those who were too frail or infirm to come to the school, the school would go to them. School children were often sent to the Old Folk's Centers, to visit, to learn and, in Hannah chan's case, to share a cup of green tea.

Ancient gravestones

CHAPTER 21

GETTING READY FOR SWIMMING LESSONS

The only thing that Hannah didn't like about gym class was that the boys and girls had to get changed into their gym clothes in the classroom right in front of each other. Though the other kids didn't seem to mind stripping down to their underwear in class, it was something that Hannah did not like one bit!

"Don't you think it's weird, Mom, boys and girls having to get changed in the same room?" she asked Mother one day.

Hannah was very excited when she left for school that morning. It was the first day of swimming lessons.

"Do you have everything you need?" asked Mother.

"Yes Mom," replied Hannah.

"Do you have your bathing cap?"

"Yes Mom."

"Do you have your swimsuit? Your goggles?"

"Yes Mom. I have everything."

"You've got your thermos and your changing towel?" asked Mother, mentally ticking off the list in her head. "Oh, and what about that little wooden thingamajig?"

"Yes, yes Mom!" replied Hannah, exhaling noisily through her nostrils. "See you, I've got to go. They're already coming down the street, see you, bye," said Hannah, flinging her heavy backpack across her shoulder as she headed out the door.

"*Mom…I'm okay*" said Hannah under her breath, looking back and motioning stiffly to Mother to get back inside and to leave her alone. Hannah had told Mother before *not* to stand in the doorway when she was on her way to school. "It's embarrassing! Everyone is watching me! Why can't you just wait inside?" she had said.

For the most part, Mother had respected that request. But every now and then her concern or perhaps her curiosity had simply overpowered her. She watched as the little group of school children turned the corner and disappeared from sight.

Mother had spent much of last weekend finding and putting together the supplies that Hannah had needed for today, the first day of swimming lessons. Nothing, of course, could be found on Iwagi-jima and so Mother was obliged to look off the island. She found the changing towels in a small department store at Innoshima. Taro and Hannah had each picked out their own design. They looked up at the store mannequins displaying the towels and tried to figure out how, exactly, to use this new device.

"Hmm…I want a really long one," said Taro.

"What for Taro?…you don't need a long one. You only have to put it up to your waist. I need the long one! I have to put it up to my shoulders," said Hannah.

"Oh, I guess you are right. So how do you change in it?" Taro asked his sister. "Where do you put your hands?"

"Underneath. You stick your hands underneath and pull off your clothes first and then you put on your swim suit," explained Hannah.

The clever change towel was shaped like a tube with stretchy elastic at one end and snap buttons from top to bottom.

GETTING READY FOR SWIMMING LESSONS

"Okay... but when I get out of the pool, I'm wet, right!? So how do I take off my swimsuit and dry off at the same time with one towel? It doesn't make sense," said Taro.

"Well, I guess you should dry off first. Use it as a normal towel first and then get changed," said Hannah.

"Good idea, Hannah!" replied Taro. "But what if all the snaps pop open while I'm getting changed. *Then* what am I going to do?" asked Taro.

"Yaa, you're right, Taro. I don't know. Can that happen, Mom?" asked Hannah.

The children were very concerned with the changing process. No longer would they be stripping down to just their underwear. It was worse than that. They would be naked! Mother, who was as confused as they were, replied confidently, "Well, we know that that won't happen because there is an elastic and the elastic is stretchy so there is no pressure on the snaps to open, right!?"

"Well, what are the snaps for then?" asked Hannah.

"I guess that when you are not using the towel as a change room you can use it as a normal towel or as a blanket if you want to," responded Mother.

"Oh, I get it," said Hannah.

"Yaa, you're right," said Taro.

"So, have you got the ones you want?" asked Mother, who was now acutely aware of the curious eyes peering at them from behind the racks of clothes.

"I'll take this one," said Taro.

"Hmm. I think I'll get this one, with the dolphins," said Hannah.

The children, oblivious to the other shoppers, each handed Mother their chosen towels.

"Thanks Mom," they said together.

CHAPTER 22

SWIMMING LESSONS

It was after five and Taro and Hannah had still not returned from school. Mother was anxious to hear how the first swimming lesson had gone. It had been a scorchingly hot and humid day on Iwagi. The season was brutal. Even the locals were complaining. "*Mushi atsui desu ne*—very muggy," they would say, mopping their brows as they greeted their neighbours in the streets.

For Mother, having to cook was the worst. She would open her doors and windows to catch the slightest movement of air and would aim the two fans directly at her face. With the doors open, the flies and mosquitoes buzzed around her bare arms and legs. She cooked and sweated and slapped her way through the dinner preparations. With all the noise from the fans, Mother didn't hear the children when they entered the *genkan*.

"We're home," yelled Taro and Hannah.

"Can I have a drink. I am *so* thirsty!" said Taro.

"Me too, Mom, I'm dying of thirst!"

Mother turned off the hot plate, got some drinks from the refrigerator, and went into the tatami mat room. It was the only room in the house that had an air conditioner. It was cool, and pleasant and without mosquitoes.

"So, how did it all work out today?" asked Mother.

"Taro couldn't go," said Hannah.

"What? What do you mean?"

"I couldn't go swimming because of the bandage on my knee," said Taro.

"Oh, that's a shame," said Mother.

"So, what did you do instead?" asked Mother.

"Oh, nothing," said Taro. "I just sat there."

Mother felt her heart drop a little. She never liked the children to feel disappointed or discouraged. She felt responsible for having brought them here. She quickly tried to think of something cheerful or positive to say. But before she could say anything Taro piped up.

"But it was okay, Mom. I got to look at some cool comic books. All the other kids were jealous."

Mother smiled. "So it wasn't too bad…your day?"

"No, not at all," replied Taro.

"Maybe your knee will heal soon and you can join in in a few days."

"Yaa, I guess so…. but I don't mind. I like looking at books," said Taro.

"What about you, Hannah? Did you go in the water?" asked Mother.

"Uh huh!" said Hannah. "It was sooo fun! We didn't have to do *anything* this afternoon, no work at all! It takes a long time: getting there by bus, changing, doing the lesson, getting the bus home. It took up the whole afternoon. It was great!"

"So, what was that little wooden plaque for?" asked Mother. She had been curious about the purpose of the small piece of wood that each child had to make and carry with them in their backpacks. They had to write their name, age, address and telephone number on it. It was kind of a mystery. Thank goodness, thought Mother, that Taro's and Hannah's teachers had helped to write the information on the plaque for the children.

"Oh, you mean that little wooden thing?" asked Hannah.

"Yes," replied Mother. "Did you need it? What did you do with it?"

"Well, at the beginning of class we put them out on the deck of the pool. Everybody puts theirs down. At the end of the class we pick them up and put them away in our packs."

"Oh," said Mother, still confused.

"They're so nobody drowns," explained Hannah.

"What do you mean?" asked Mother.

"You are supposed to use them whenever you go into the water, even at the beach, the teacher said. You see, they can tell if anybody's missing. If there is still a wooden piece left over then that person has drowned and then they can call their families," explained Hannah.

"Yaa," said Taro.

"Oh, I see," replied Mother giving up on the explanation.

"Oh, and Mom, we played games in the water and splashed Miyamoto sensei."

"How was the changing towel?" asked Mother.

"It was okay putting on my bathing suit, but kind of hard taking it off at the end. My body was wet and everything kept rolling up and sticking to my skin," said Hannah.

" Oh, I see," said Mother.

"It was kind of embarrassing today too, Mom," said Hannah.

" Oh, why? What happened?" asked Mother.

"Well, the girls, Moegi chan and some of the others, started to tease me."

"Huh," said Taro. "What did they do?"

"Well, when I was putting on my swimsuit, they started giggling and then they started saying 'Oh, wait til Sayaka kun sees you in your bathing suit. He's going to go, *mero, mero, mero.*"

"What does *that* mean?" asked Taro.

"You know," said Hannah, "*mero, mero, mero.*" She rolled her eyes, fluttered her arms and wobbled her knees.

"Oh, I get it!" laughed Taro. "That's mean! I would have kicked them."

"They all think he's in love with me, but I hate him. He's so creepy!" said Hannah.

"Well," said Mother, "did he?"

"Did he what?" asked Hannah.

"Go *mero, mero, mero,*" said Mother.

"Yaa, kind of," said Hannah.

CHAPTER 23

EARLY MORNING DELIVERIES

'Ping Pong.' Mother groaned. It was the door bell. It was just after five in the morning. 'Not again,' she thought to herself. The first time it had happened, the children had bolted up in their beds in alarm.

"What's that? What's going on? Is it a fire?" called out Hannah in a sleepy confused state.

"Sshh… go back to sleep," Mother had said. "It's just the door bell."

Nowadays, when it rang, the children would just grunt out: "*Mom….*" and then go back to sleep. Mother, jarred from sleep, would upright herself in bed, shake off the disorientation and rush as best she could down the steep and narrow wooden stairs yelling "*Chotto matte kudasai*—just a moment please!" She would open the front door to a broadly grinning Ikeda san.

"*Ohayo Gozaimasu,*" he said.

"*Ohayo,*" replied Mother, trying to look and sound as if she had already been awake for awhile. She always felt a little embarrassed answering the door with disheveled hair and night clothes, like she was lazy for sleeping so late. Ikeda san smiled and proudly handed Mother a bag.

"I've been up to the *hatake* this morning," he said. "And I found some *kuwagata* and *kabutomushi* for Taro kun and Hannah chan."

"*Waa, sugoi! Arigato*—wow, that's great! Thank you." Mother feigned excitement and thanked Mr. Ikeda profusely in the best Japanese she could put together at that time in the morning.

"*Jaa, mata ne*—well, I'll see you later," said Ikeda san.

"*Arigato*," replied Mother, taking the bag, bowing and closing the door. She deposited the bag in the *genkan,* used the washroom and headed back up the stairs to her bed.

It was difficult getting back to sleep. Mother knew that in just a few minutes the Iwagi morning announcements would begin. They would be broadcast by loudspeaker across the island. It would start with morning bells and then loud distorted voices blaring important news for the day: changes in ferry schedules, school events, typhoon forecasts. After that Mother could hear the neighbours coughing and clearing their throats. The day on Iwagijima had begun. Soon the whirring of washing machines in the courtyards could be heard and she knew it was time for her too to start the day. Mother went downstairs to prepare breakfast.

"Taro, Hannah, breakfast time! Time to get up!" yelled Mother up the stairs. She waited for a few minutes while she set out their breakfasts on the low table and then tried again. " Come on you guys, get up, your breakfasts are getting cold."

Taro was first. He came down the stairs, used the washroom and headed towards the tatami room

"What's for breakfast Mom?"

"Miso soup, rice and scrambled eggs," replied Mother.

"Yum," said Taro as he picked up a comic book and began to eat his breakfast.

"Milk or juice?" asked Mother.

"Juice please."

EARLY MORNING DELIVERIES

"Would you like *takuwan*—japanese pickles?" asked Mother.

"Oh, yes please," replied Taro.

Taro had always preferred rice to bread and salty to sweet. It was in his genes, Father had said. Mother would often tell friends the story of when Taro was a baby. How he would be looking through a picture book. When he came across a colourful fish or sea creature, he would point to it and say: 'It looks delicious!' While most other toddlers, including his sister, would say the fish was cute or pretty, Taro would want to eat it. 'It's genetic,' Father would say to Mother, "Nature over nurture."

Hannah slid open the door. Rubbing her sleepy eyes, she sat down at the table.

"Could I have a glass of milk please, Mom?" She took a bite of her thick, white, toast slathered with strawberry jam.

After the children had finished their breakfast, Mother said, "If you hurry and get ready for school I'll give you a surprise."

"A surprise?" asked Hannah. "What do you mean? What kind of a surprise?"

"Yaa, what is it, Mom? Is it a new game for my Gameboy?' asked Taro, full of hope.

"What, Mom! Taro got a new game!? That's not fair! What did I get, Mom?"

"No, no, stop! It's not that kind of a surprise," sighed Mother.

"Oh," said Taro, his voice dropping. "What is it then?"

"It's in the *genkan*, in a bag," said Mother.

"Oh, I know," said Hannah.

"What. What is it?" asked Taro.

"Ikeda san came this morning, didn't he, Mom? Remember, Taro."

"Oh, I get it," said Taro.

Hannah and Taro ran to the *genkan*. Hannah snatched up the bag first.

"Let's see, Hannah," said Taro, reaching over impatiently to take the bag.

"*Ta a a ro*! I've got it! Let me open it!" said Hannah.

Hannah opened the bag and they both peered inside.

"Beetles!"

"Let's put them in our box," said Taro. The bug box was kept just outside the *genkan* door.

"Okay," said Hannah. "I'll open the lid and you put them in." Hannah sat down on the stoop, lifted the heavy stones off the top of the large, see through plastic cage and slid off the lid. The heavy stones were used to keep the alley cats from pushing it over.

"Look Hannah, two *kabutomushi*—rhinocerous beetles, and they're big too," said Taro. "Sweet! Look at this one. We've got a *nokogiri*. Look Hannah , it's the same as the one in the book."

"*Cool*!" said Hannah. "That one is mine, okay Taro? You can have the *kabutomushi*."

"No… that's not fair!" protested Taro.

"Yes! You got the biggest *kuwagata* yesterday Taro, remember?"

"Oh, alright Hannah! Geez," said Taro as he placed it into the case.

"Oh, oh, look Hannah," said Taro. "Zoe's dead!"

"Oh," said Hannah, her voice dropping.

Taro reached in and pulled out the dead beetle. He tossed it into the lane. The children had given names to the beetles, the names of their friends at school in Canada.

"What about Max and Madison? Are they still alive?" asked Hannah.

Taro poked at two of the beetles with a long thin stick. "Yup, They're okay," he said as he watched them scurry away.

"Oh, good," said Hannah. "Let's have a battle."

"Okay," said Taro. "I'll choose Alex." He put his hand in and pulled out a medium sized *kabutomushi*.

EARLY MORNING DELIVERIES

"Hmm, I think I'll pick Madison. She's strong!" Hannah pulled out a larger *kuwagata* and examined the horns. "Okay, I'm ready. Let's start. *Ichi, ni, no san*—one, two, three!" yelled Hannah. Both children put down their beetles on the pavement, almost on top of each other. They watched as the two beetles locked horns and pushed.

"*Yes*!" yelled Taro as Alex flipped Madison over onto her back. They continued to watch.

"Taro, Hannah, what are you up to? The kids'll be here any minute."

"We're having a battle," said Hannah.

"Yes, I can see that," answered Mother. "Well, you better put them back in their cage and wash up your hands."

"Oh," grumbled Taro. "Alex was winning."

"No," protested Hannah.

The children put away their beetles and replaced the large stones. They washed their hands and headed out the door, just in time to join their group for the walk to school.

Fighting beetles

CHAPTER 24

TARO AND HANNAH

Although they weren't the common family pet in Canada, the children very much enjoyed their box of battling beetles. They also liked playing with, and especially feeding, their two pet turtles. Unlike the beetles, who were named after their Canadian school mates, the turtles they named after themselves.

Taro and *Hannah* were the very smallest of the turtles that Ikeda san had brought over in buckets in the back of his truck. They now resided in a small aquarium on the ledge in the *genkan*. They had at the beginning been placed outside the front door, beside the beetles, but the neighbourhood cats would not leave them alone.

Hannah and Taro had worked hard to set up a home for their turtles. They had collected water from the stream. They had found a large stone and placed it inside the aquarium to make an island. The two turtles liked to rest on top of the large stone.

"What do they eat, Mom?" asked Hannah.

"I'm not sure?" replied Mother. "Maybe you should try to find some bugs to feed them. Maybe they eat flies or worms."

Mother, who had never owned turtles before as pets had no idea how to take care of them.

"Here," said Mother, handing Taro the bug catching box. "Why don't you and Hannah go and find some food?"

"Come on, Taro. I know what they'll eat," said Hannah.

"What, Hannah? What do they eat?" asked Taro.

"Come on, I'll show you," she said.

And off they went, down the lane in search of food for their turtles. They returned about half an hour later, hot and discouraged.

"So, what did you get?" asked Mother.

"It was stupid," said Taro. "We couldn't find anything!"

"Yes, we did, Mom. Look," said Hannah. "We got an ant and a grasshopper."

"Oh, that's stupid," said Taro. "They won't eat that!"

"How do you know?" said Hannah. "Let's put them in and see."

"Oh, alright!" said Taro. "But they're not going to eat it!"

Mother helped the children carry the aquarium from the ledge to the outside. They sat down on the stoop and peered in the top. *Taro* and *Hannah* turtle, having been upset by the sudden movement, were swimming around frantically. Eventually, they climbed onto their island and settled down.

"I'll put the grasshopper in, Taro. You put in the ant," said Hannah. "Put yours in first," she said.

Taro nimbly snatched up the large ant between his thumb and forefinger and placed it on top of the island. The children waited. The ant circled madly but neither turtle made a move for it. They just sat there.

"Put in the grasshopper," said Taro. "Maybe they want that!"

Hannah opened the box, grabbed the grasshopper and quickly placed it on the middle of the stone. The turtles, startled, dove into the water. The grasshopper bounded up into the air, almost hitting Hannah in the face. Hannah screamed!

"Catch it, Taro," she yelled.

TARO AND HANNAH

Taro lurched after it, catching the grasshopper on its third leap. He grabbed it with both hands.

"You've got to stick it into the water!" he said. "You can't put it on the rock!"

This time, instead of placing it on the rock, Taro plunged it into the depths. The grasshopper flailed about in the water. The turtles, took shelter and hid partly submerged on the far side of the island.

"See, I told you, Hannah! This is useless. It's not going to work," said Taro.

"Maybe they're not hungry," said Hannah.

"Yaa, right!" said Taro.

Mother, who could see the frustration, knew that a quarrel was about to erupt.

"I've got an idea," she said. "I'm making *ma bo dofu* tonight for supper. I have some raw hamburger in the fridge. Shall we try that?"

"Yaa, let's try that," said Hannah. "They might like that."

"I doubt it!" said Taro.

Mother brought out a spoonful of raw hamburger along with a couple of toothpicks.

"Why don't we put some onto the rock?" said Mother.

"Oh, can I do it?" asked Hannah.

"Sure," said Mother. "Just make sure you wash your hands well afterwards. Raw hamburger can make you quite sick."

Hannah, using the toothpick, carefully poked some of the raw hamburger off of the spoon and onto the rock. They waited quietly, peering into the top of the aquarium.

"Look!" whispered Hannah. "*Taro* is starting to move towards the hamburger."

"Huh?!" said Taro. "You're right, Hannah!"

"Sshh, sshh," whispered Mother. "Don't scare them."

Mother and the children waited and watched quietly.

"Look!" said Taro. "*Hannah's* moving towards it too!"

Taro kept moving closer and closer to the small pile of hamburger. *Hannah* was following close behind.

"He's eating it!" yelled Taro. "Look Mom, *Taro's* eating the hamburger!"

"Oh, oh, here comes *Hannah*. She's eating it, too!" cried out Hannah.

"Hooray!" shouted the children.

"We need more, Mom," said Taro.

Mother poked a big glump of hamburger onto the rock. *Hannah* dove at it, pushing *Taro* out of her way, and began wolfing down the raw meat. The children laughed in delight.

"What a pig you are, Hannah!" said Taro.

CHAPTER 25

FRUIT PICKING

Ikeda san loved children. And there was nothing he liked better than to teach Taro and Hannah about the Iwagi of his childhood. He came often to the house early on weekend mornings to take Mother and the children off on an adventure.

"Get up, Taro, Hannah. Get dressed," said Mother gently one morning.

"Huh, what? What's going on?" asked Taro. "It's the weekend. What do we have to get up for? I want to sleep in!"

"Sshh…..just get up," said Mother. "Ikeda san is waiting outside."

"Huh? What? Oh no," said Taro. "Where are we going now?" he asked. "I just want to sleep in, to stay home!"

"Mom," said Hannah groggily. "Can we go later? *Pleeaase*! Do we *have* to go? Where are we going anyways?"

"I'm not sure," replied Mother.

"What?! What do you mean?" asked Taro.

"Well," said Mother. "I'm not really sure. I couldn't quite understand what Ikeda san was saying. But I know it will be fun! Come on. Let's get ready," encouraged Mother. She too, would have liked to sleep in. But on the other hand, she felt grateful to Mr. Ikeda. After all, it was because of him that they were all learning so much about living on Iwagijima.

Mother hurriedly reheated the *miso* soup and scooped some warm rice from the rice cooker into bowls. She placed them on the table.

"Can I have toast instead?" asked Hannah.

Mother looked at her watch. They had to leave in ten minutes. "Hmm, how about I make you a deal, Hannah? How about you eat this now and I'll make you a grilled cheese sandwich when we get home. Okay?"

"Okay, I guess so," said Hannah. Can I have a coke float too….. later, as a special treat?" she asked. She knew that she was in a prime bargaining position.

"A coke float? Yaa, me too. I want one too," said Taro.

"Alright," said Mother. "But hurry up and get ready. Brush your teeth. When you're done we've got to go."

Mother was just cleaning off the table and putting the dishes into the sink when the doorbell rang. 'Ping Pong.' Hannah went to open the door.

"*Ohayo*, Hannah chan," said Mr. Ikeda.

"*Ohayo*," replied Hannah.

"*Domo, domo*," said Mother as she hurried the children out of the house and locked the door. They followed Mr. Ikeda up the alley to where his small truck was waiting for them. They squeezed in.

"Are we going to the *hatake* again, Mom?" asked Taro.

"I don't know," replied Mother. "We'll just have to wait and see."

One of the things Mother liked about Japan was that she didn't have to always make small talk. It was okay to just look out the window. In the beginning, when Mother had first come to Japan, she felt the silent spaces to be awkward and uncomfortable. But after awhile she relaxed and enjoyed the fact that she didn't always have to talk. And with her limited language ability, the custom of silence was a blessing.

"Taro kun, Hannah chan, *biwa tabetta koto ga aru*—Have you ever tasted *biwa*?" asked Ikeda san.

FRUIT PICKING

"No, I don't think so," replied Hannah.

"Have we ever eaten *biwa*, Mom?" she asked.

"I don't know," replied Mother. "I'm not sure what *biwa* is," she said.

Mother cursed herself for forgetting to bring her dictionary. Usually, when Mother went off on an adventure with the children she would bring along a backpack with drinks, snacks, tissues, band aids and a dictionary. She had been in such a rush this morning that she had forgotten everything except for a water bottle.

Ikeda san continued up a mountain path. At the top of the path, he pulled over and parked his truck beside a house. He got out of his truck and went over to greet an elderly man and woman who were pruning some bushes. Taro and Hannah and Mother climbed out of the truck, too. The elderly couple smiled at them. "*Domo, domo,*" they said.

Ikeda san reached into the back of his pick-up, pulled out a bucket and handed it to Hannah. He reached in again and pulled out a long metal pole with clippers on the top. The elderly gentleman was pointing up to the side of the mountain. Ikeda san bowed. "*Domo, domo,*" he said. Mother and the children followed behind.

Soon, an orchard of fruit trees could be seen on the side of the hill.

"These are *biwa,*" explained Ikeda. He plucked one off of a branch, peeled off the skin and bit into the flesh. "*Oishii—delicious!*" he said. He pulled off three more *biwa* and gave one each to Taro, Hannah, and Mother.

"*Dozo, tabette kudasai! Please try it.*"

The fruit was yellow in color, with a thin skin. It looked like a small mango.

"Mmmm, juicy!" said Taro after taking a bite. "*Oishii!*"

"*Oishii,*" said Hannah to Ikeda san.

Ikeda san smiled and motioned for Mother and the children to pick as much fruit as they liked. He showed Taro and Hannah how to pick the *biwa*. It was important, he said, not to remove the stem.

"Oh, boy!" said Taro. "Hannah, you hold the bucket and I'll pick the fruit and hand it to you."

"No! I want to pick the fruit too," said Hannah.

"I'll hold the bucket!" said Mother.

Mother took the bucket from Hannah. She bit into her piece of fruit. Taro was right. It was sweet and juicy. Mother had never tasted it before. It was delicious!

The children filled the bucket in no time and then they started to fill their mouths. They chose the ripest and the plumpest. And they ate. One, after another, after another. After about twenty minutes, they started acting silly.

"Oh, yuck! This one isn't ripe," said Taro, after taking one bite from the *biwa* he had in his hand. He tossed the fruit at Hannah.

"Hey! What are you doing?" she asked. "You wait!" Hannah plucked another one off of her tree and bit into it.

"Eeooo! This is too sour," she said and threw it at Taro. It hit him smack in the shoulder.

"Hey," said Taro.

Soon the children were at it. Laughing and pelting each other with *biwa*. Mother looked on helplessly.

"Stop it!" she said. "You are being very disrespectful. You are wasting the fruit. Stop it now!"

The children stopped their game and looked down and away from Mother's gaze.

"Taro started it!" said Hannah.

"Did not!" said Taro.

"Stop it. I said stop it!" yelled Mother. "It is a good thing that Ikeda san didn't see you."

With their heads low, the children climbed down from the hillside in silence. They walked with Mother back along the path towards the house. The elderly gentleman and Ikeda san were waiting.

FRUIT PICKING

"How was it?" asked Ikeda.

"*Tanoshikatta*—It was fun!" said Hannah.

"*Unh*—yes," said Taro.

The old grandmother came out from the house carrying something in her hands. She smiled at the children and handed each of them an ice cream bar. "*Dozo*," she said.

"*Arigato*," said the children.

~ ❦ ~

Later that evening, after the children had gone to bed, Mother made herself a cup of tea and sat down at the low table. She opened her dictionary. She flipped through the pages until she found the word *biwa*. *Biwa*, it said, was a fruit. In English it is called loquat. Mother scratched her head. She had never seen or tasted a loquat before today. She took a sip of her tea. She looked out onto the covered porch. Now, besides the bulging boxes of onions and the giant crate of potatoes, stood two buckets overflowing with loquats. She smiled as she recalled Ikeda san dropping them off at home earlier in the day with the two big buckets of fruit.

"Be sure to keep them in the refrigerator," he had said.

CHAPTER 26

THE THERMOS

A lot of things were different at Iwagi Shogakko. For example, there was the routine of emptying your school backpack when you first arrived in the classroom. In Canada, Hannah and her classmates simply flung their backpacks higgledy piggledy onto hooks at the back of the room. Zippers would be left half unzipped, lunch bags would be left hanging out. Although teachers would admonish the children and tell them to keep things neat, they paid little heed. Hannah could not get away with such lax behavior at Iwagi Shogakko.

"Boy, are they ever strict at school," said Hannah one day. "Everything has to be perfect. First, you have to unpack your school bag and put all of your books into your desk. Then, you have to take it and put it into the cubby hole at the back of the class. It *has* to be empty. The flap *has* to be facing out and you *have to* put your hat on top, like this," said Hannah, showing Mother how to place the hat on top of the yellow school bag just so.

"What do you do with your thermos?" asked Mother.

"Oh, the thermos. Well, you hang it over the back of your chair. You are allowed to drink from it whenever you like. At least that's one good thing!" said Hannah. "Oh, yaa, and I want water in my thermos from now on. You wouldn't believe what happened to me today, Mom. It was so embarrassing!"

"Embarrassing?" repeated Mother. "What happened?"

"Oh, my gosh…. I didn't know what to do, Mom," continued Hannah. "I almost got caught with my thermos!"

"What do you mean? Caught with your thermos. You're allowed to have a thermos, aren't you?" asked Mother.

"Yes, we always use our thermos. That's okay. But, well, you see, we had gym class right after lunch today, right?" said Hannah.

"Uh huh, and…." said Mother.

"Well, we were running around outside and playing games, right?" said Hannah.

"Right," said Mother, wondering where the story was heading.

"Well, it's hot outside, right?"

"Right," said Mother.

"Well, when we got back inside the classroom, everybody was sweating like crazy. And we all sat down and took big gulps from our thermoses," said Hannah.

"Yes," said Mother. "So, I don't get it. What happened?"

"Well, I was drinking from my thermos, right, when Kana chan looked over at me and said, 'Hannah chan, can I have some of yours? I'm so thirsty and I don't have any left, " recounted Hannah.

"So," said Mother. "What's wrong with that?"

"*MOM* ………! Don't you remember? I didn't have water or tea in my thermos. I had juice! You're not allowed to have juice in your thermos."

"Oh, I see," said Mother, finally understanding Hannah's predicament. "So, what did you do?"

"That's just it! I didn't know what to do. I couldn't let her have any or else she would know and then I would get in trouble," explained Hannah.

THE THERMOS

"So, what *did* you do?" asked Mother.

"Well, she was reaching over for it so I said, 'I don't have any left.' But then she said, 'let me see.' So I said, 'well, there's a little left but I have a bad cold and I can't let you drink from it.' "

"Quick thinking, Hannah!" said Mother.

"But, I don't think she believed me," said Hannah. "My face felt all hot and prickly. I was so embarrassed. I could have been in big trouble! I'm not bringing juice in my thermos to school anymore!" said Hannah. "Okay, Mom?"

CHAPTER 27

BOSSES FOR THE DAY

Father was surprised that evening when Hannah chan asked him to please cut her finger nails.

"That's not like you, Hannah," said Father, who usually had to chase her around the house and finally trap her to get the job done. Father smiled. Then he said, "Sure. Come on, sit down over here and I will cut them for you."

Hannah walked over towards Father and sat down.

"Do it gently," she said. "I don't want it to hurt." Hannah continued, "I get to be '*Nichokusan*' tomorrow," explained Hannah.

"Oh," said Father. "Hmmm, I can see why you need these trimmed, they're awful," he said, looking at her long, dirty, ragged nails.

"*D-a-a-d!*" protested Hannah.

"So, what is it you get to be tomorrow?" he asked Hannah.

"*Nichokusan*," said Hannah. "Kana chan and I get to be *Nichokusan*."

"What's that?" asked Father.

"Well," said Hannah. "*Nichokusan* is kind of like 'bosses for the day.'"

"Oh," said Father. "Bosses for the day. That sounds interesting. Do you get to boss around Sayaka kun and Moegi chan?" he asked.

"*D-a-a-d!* Stop teasing me!" said Hannah.

"Well, what do you get to do when you are the boss?"

"You get to do all kinds of things, like writing important stuff on the blackboard and you get to lead the class throughout the day. Like, when Miyamoto sensei comes in, the *Nichokusans* stand up at the front of the class."

"Yes.... and then what?" encouraged Father.

"Well, and then we make everybody stand up and follow us, like this." Hannah stood up tall with her hands straight down by her sides. "*Kiritsu kiotsuke re*," she said and took a deep, stiff, bow. "*Hajimemasho*! That means, now we are going to start the class. We do stuff like that when we start and when we finish. And oh yaa, at lunch time, the bosses stand in front of the class, like this." Hannah demonstrated by standing straight with her hands together in a kind of praying position. "We say, '*te wo awasette*,' that means, did everybody wash their hands? And then, the class says, '*Hai, awaseimashita*'—Yes we did! After that everybody together says '*itadakimasu*—let's eat,' and the bosses say '*dozo*.' And then we all get to eat!" said Hannah.

Father smiled. He was very impressed by Hannah's growing command of the Japanese language and especially proud of her newly found confidence.

"That's great!" he said. "But I have just one question."

"Yaa, what is it Dad?" asked Hannah.

"Why did you want me to cut your fingernails?"

"Oh," replied Hannah softly. "Well, you see, sometimes Miyamoto sensei checks our fingernails to see if they are clean," she explained. "And since I am the boss tomorrow, I don't want to be embarrassed or make any mistakes," said Hannah.

"Oh, I see," said Father.

CHAPTER 28

TARO'S FIGHT

It was about four o'clock when the children got home from school that day. It had been another very hot and sticky day on Iwagi. Mother had already been to the supermarket. She had bought some sticks of yakitori and a delicious looking wedge of watermelon. She had put it into the refrigerator so it would be nice and cold for the afternoon snack.

"Hi guys," greeted Mother. "You look hot! Let me help you with your stuff." Mother helped Hannah off with her heavy school bag.

"I'm hungry," said Hannah. "What's for snack?"

"I've got something really good," responded Mother.

"Oh boy what is it, Mom?" asked Hannah.

"Well, sit down and you'll see. I'll bring it to you."

Mother noticed that Taro did not seem his usual self. After all, it was mostly Taro who took interest in what snack time offered, not Hannah.

"Are you hungry, Taro?" asked Mother.

"Yaa… I guess so," he said in a soft voice.

"Is everything okay?" asked Mother. "Was school alright today?"

"Well, not really…." answered Taro.

Mother could feel her heart sink. Taro, unlike Hannah, kept most of his problems inside. He did not often talk about things that bothered him. Mother prodded gently.

"So…were you feeling a little sick?" she asked.

"No," he said. "It's not that. I had some problems with some kids."

"Oh," said Mother, feeling a pang deep in her stomach. "Were some of them mean to you?" she asked.

"Yaa, kind of, I guess," said Taro.

Hannah's ears perked up instantly. "What happened? What did they do? Who was it?" asked Hannah.

"Oh, I don't know," said Taro. "It's just that they …. they want me to fight them."

Mother felt another dull stab. "Who wants to fight?"

"The boys in my class," replied Taro

"All the boys?" asked Mother.

"No, not all of them," said Taro. "There's this one kid, Kenji, who always bugs me at school."

"What does he do?" asked Mother.

"Oh, I don't know. He does stuff like rub my head or pushes me. He imitates me a lot, too. He tries to get everybody to laugh at me."

"Oh, I see," said Mother. "He sounds like a bit of a bully. Does your teacher know?"

"Well, he usually does it when she's not in the class," said Taro.

"So, what do you do when he does that?" asked Mother.

"Oh, nothing. I just try to ignore him. I don't know why he hates me so much. I never did anything to him," said Taro.

"You should just beat him up, Taro," interjected Hannah. "You could, you know!"

"Yaa, I know but…"

"Is he the one that wants to fight you?" interrupted Mother.

"Well, he's one of them. There's a few others too," said Taro.

Mother was starting to become alarmed. She had heard that bullying was a problem in Japan. "Maybe I should go and talk to your teacher," said Mother. "Does Ikeuchi sensei know about the kids wanting you to fight them?" she asked.

"Yaa, well she sort of does…" said Taro.

"And what does she say," asked Mother.

"Well, I kind of talked to her and she said I should just fight them," said Taro.

"Oh," said Mother, not quite knowing what else to say. She knew that in Canada teachers would never give children that kind of advice. In fact, fighting with classmates could easily get a child expelled from school. Teachers would always say, 'You've got to use your words,' encouraging children to talk their way through a problem rather than getting physical. Taro interrupted her thoughts.

"She said that if I didn't fight them then they would keep bugging and bugging me. She said that if I did fight then they'd probably leave me alone."

"Oh," said Mother.

"I don't really want to fight anybody. I don't like fighting. But, I guess I have to," said Taro.

'I'll help you," said Hannah. " I hate those guys. Especially that stupid little Kenji. Anyway, Taro, you should just pound him. Then he'll leave you alone. Right, Mom?"

Mother could feel an anger welling up inside her. "Yaa, you're right, Hannah. One swift kick to the head, Taro, that's all it'd take. That's what I would do."

Mother calmed herself down and having regained her composure she continued. "But, Taro, has to do what he feels comfortable with," she said.

"I don't want to get into trouble, Mom. In Canada, we get into big trouble for fighting," he said.

"But you know, Taro, I don't think you'd get into trouble here. Remember, you did ask your teacher and what did she say to do?" continued Mother.

"She said I should fight them," said Taro.

Taro remained rather subdued for the rest of that day.

༺☙༻

The next morning Taro and Hannah left for school as usual. Mother gave Taro a hug. "Don't worry too much, Taro. Things'll work out," she said. "Hannah, you watch out for him, okay?"

"I will Mom," replied Hannah.

Mother tried not to worry about Taro during the day. But no matter where she was or what she was doing, hanging out laundry, vacuuming, shopping for groceries, her mind always drifted back to Taro. She tried to block out images of bullying and taunting. She tried to block out visions of a beat up Taro, lying bleeding on the school's gravel field. 'Maybe, I should ride up to the school on my bicycle and wait for him to come out,' she thought to herself. 'No....I'll just wait. I'll wait and see.'

When five o'clock rolled around and neither Taro nor Hannah had returned from school, Mother became anxious. 'I wonder what I should do. If they are not back within the next five minutes I *will* go out and look for them,' she decided. Suddenly, Mother's ears picked up the sound of the children down the lane. She rushed to the door, a little afraid of what she might see.

"Taro, Hannah," she called. "Where *were* you? It's after five." Mother quickly glanced at Taro. He didn't look beat up.

"We got to pick our instruments for band today, after school. That's why we're so late," said Hannah. "I picked the trumpet," she said.

"Oh, that should be fun," said Mother.

She took another quick look at Taro. He wasn't limping. He seemed fine.

TARO'S FIGHT

"How about you, Taro, what did you pick?" asked Mother.

"Oh," said Taro. "I'm going to play the drum."

"Great!" said Mother.

The children came into the house and sat down in the tatami room at the low table.

"What's for snack? I'm starving," said Taro.

"Well, how about a croquette. I bought some at the supermarket. I'll heat them up for you."

Mother prepared the croquettes and placed them on the table with two glasses of juice and a bottle of ketchup.

"So… how did it go today, Taro? With Kenji? Did anything happen?" asked Mother.

"Oh, it was fine, Mom," responded Taro.

"Did they still want to fight you?" asked Mother.

Hannah interrupted. "Oh Mom, you see, Taro told me what happened, he…"

"Hannah, it's okay. It's Taro's story. Let him tell it," said Mother, cutting Hannah off in mid sentence.

"Yes, they did," said Taro.

Mother couldn't understand why he seemed to be in such a good mood.

"So, what exactly happened, Taro?" she asked.

"He pounded him!" said Hannah.

'No I didn't Hannah," said Taro.

Taro continued. "Well, after lunch, after the teacher left, Kenji and a couple of other kids came up to me," said Taro.

"So, was it Kenji who wanted to fight?" asked Mother.

"No, not exactly," replied Taro. "Kenji pushed this other, bigger, kid, Masaaki, out to fight me."

"Boy, what a chicken that Kenji is, huh Taro," said Hannah.

"And, so, did you fight this big kid?" asked Mother.

"Well, I was going to… and we started to and he started to come towards me and then when he got really close, I, I, I gave a really fast kick to his face."

"Whoa," said Mother. "And so ….what did he do then? Where were the other kids?"

"Oh, the other kids…… they were just standing back watching. Well, when I gave this kick to his face …"

Mother interrupted. "Did you hit him?" she asked.

"Well, not exactly," replied Taro. "I stopped my kick right in front of his nose."

"Show me, Taro!" cried Hannah. "Show me how you did it!"

Hannah stood up. Taro stood up.

"Like this, Hannah," said Taro. Taro gave a swift, precise kick. The air whipped around his foot, which stopped a hair's breadth from Hannah's face.

"Wow……" said Hannah. "That's amazing!" "So what did he do, Taro? Did he fight back?"

"No…. he didn't," said Taro.

"So what happened," asked Mother.

"Oh, nothing," replied Taro. "He just started backing away. He started saying: '*Tsuyoi, tsuyoi*—you're too strong! I'm not going to fight you.' "

"Yay!" yelled Hannah. "Yay, Taro!"

"Good for you, Taro! Aren't you happy you have those skills?" said Mother.

"I bet they didn't know you had a Black Belt did they Taro?" asked Hannah.

"No, I don't think they did. But they do now!" said Taro.

"So, were they still mean to you after that?" asked Mother.

"No, not at all," replied Taro. "They were all really nice to me."

Mother walked over to Taro and wrapped her arms around him. She gave him a big hug. "I'm proud of you!" she said.

CHAPTER 29

KURU KURU SUSHI

It was just after lunch on Saturday when Mr. Ikeda came by. "Come on," he said. "We're going to Innoshima for shopping."

Mother got things ready to go. She slipped two 'Calvin and Hobbes' comic books, a bottle of water and the dictionary into her backpack.

"Where are we going?" asked Hannah.

"We're going shopping on Innoshima," replied Mother. "They have a great supermarket in Innoshima," she said, "much better than the little one here in Iwagi. You wouldn't believe the selection of fish and seafood. There are hundreds and hundreds of different kinds."

"Yay!" said Taro. "Can we buy some?"

"Sure we can," replied Mother. "I just hope I can figure out how to cook it," she said.

"Is there anything else, Mom, besides fish?" asked Hannah. "I get fish everyday for my lunch at school. I don't need any more," she said.

"Oh, Hannah, I've been up there on my bicycle. They have a fantastic bakery, with beautiful little cakes too. It's not only fish. They have everything!" said Mother.

"Well, if Taro gets fish then I want cake," said Hannah.

"I get cake too, Mom!" demanded Taro.

"Alright, alright, we can get cake but we can't get too much stuff because remember, I don't have any room in the refrigerator," said Mother.

"That's okay Mom," said Hannah. "We'll eat it fast!"

Mother locked up the door and up they headed to the top of the lane where Ikeda san was waiting with his elderly mother. Mr. Ikeda had brought his car. *Obaachan*—grandmother, was sitting in the middle of the back seat. Hannah and Taro climbed in on either side of her. *Obaachan* beamed. She immediately began chatting with the children. Hannah looked up at Mother for help. Mother winked and smiled back at her from the front seat. After only a few minutes had passed Hannah tried again.

"Mom, could I have my 'Calvin and Hobbes' book please?" she asked.

Mother dug into her backpack, pulled out the comic book and handed it back to Hannah. Mother knew that Hannah was trying to hide from *Obaachan's* conversation in Japanese. But it didn't work. Mother chuckled to herself when she glanced into the backseat again and saw *Obaachan* peering intently at Hannah's book.

"What is that?" asked *Obaachan*. "What does that say?"

When Ikeda san arrived at the ferry terminal, Hannah asked if she could get out and walk around for a few minutes until the ferry arrived.

"*Dozo*," said Mr. Ikeda.

Hannah jumped out of the car. "Come on, Taro," she said. "Let's see if we can find any fish off of the dock."

Finally, they arrived at Innoshima. Ikeda san parked his car in the supermarket parking lot and they went in. The supermarket was a bustle of activity. Aside from the regular aisles of groceries there were small stalls and stands set up all along the front of the store.

"*Irrashai, rashai, rashai*," welcomed the men who were grilling or frying or steaming the many snacks. It was like a festival! There were octopus balls and sticks of grilled squid. There were hot, sweet bean pancakes in the shape of fish and steamed meat buns. The smells wafted through the air. It was too much for Taro.

"I'm hungry," he said. "Can I get something to eat?"

Mother arranged a meeting time and place with Ikeda san.

"*Dozo, yukuri,*" he said. "Please enjoy and take your time."

Obaachan smiled and bowed and off they went.

"Can I get some *takoyaki*-octopus balls," asked Taro.

"Sure," replied Mother. "What would you like, Hannah?"

"I like those steamed pizza buns. Can I get one of those?" she asked.

"Sure," said Mother. "Let's see what we can find."

After their snacks, Mother and the children wandered through the aisles of the supermarket. They marvelled at all of the different varieties of fish.

"It's like an aquarium in here, Mom!" said Hannah.

"Yaa, but they're all dead," laughed Taro.

Mother let each of the children pick one special item to put into her basket. Taro chose a package of grilled eel. It was still warm. Hannah picked out a box of 'Hello Kitty' strawberry cream cookies.

Mother continued to shop for groceries while Taro and Hannah raced around the store, stopping here and there to pick up a myriad of free samples along the way. Finally, they plunked themselves down in front of a magazine and comic book stand. It was there, about half an hour later, that Mother, Mr. Ikeda and *Obaachan* found them.

"*Ikimashooka*—Shall we go?" asked Ikeda.

"*Hai, ikimashoo*—Yes, let's go," replied Taro.

Obaachan and Mr. Ikeda were laden with bags of groceries. He opened the trunk and placed them inside along with Mother's one bag.

"We are going to visit my daughter Yuko and her family and then we will all go out for dinner," said Mr. Ikeda.

Mother and the children had not been out for dinner in a very long time. There were no restaurants on their small island of Iwagijima.

"Oh boy," said Taro. "What kind of restaurant will we go to?" he asked.

"Do you know '*Kuru Kuru Sushi*'?" asked Mr. Ikeda.

"*Kuru Kuru Sushi? I love Kuru Kuru Sushi,*" said Taro.

"What's *Kuru Kuru Sushi*?" asked Hannah.

"That's where the little plates of food go round and round in front of you and you get to pick off whichever plates you like. Remember Hannah?" asked Taro.

"Oh, I remember," said Hannah excitedly. "We did that once with Takechan in Nagoya, didn't we? And you get to stack up the plates and see how high you can go. I *love* that!" she said.

Ikeda san gave a broad smile. His eyes twinkled. He always liked it when he could please the children.

※

At about seven o'clock everyone arrived at the restaurant. They waited for a few minutes until a man called out their name. "Ikeda san!" he called.

"*Hai*," replied Mr. Ikeda. The man motioned for Ikeda san's party to take the eight seats all in a row. Hannah and Taro sat beside Yuko and her husband and their small baby boy, Yuki kun. Next was *Obaachan* then Mr. Ikeda and finally Mother sat down on the last stool. She waved to Taro and Hannah, who were sitting far away from her on the opposite end of the counter. Mother noticed that Taro had already pulled his first plate, a plate of tuna sashimi, off of the 'revolving conveyor belt.' Hannah, who was waiting for the perfect food item, watched the plates glide by. Taro had already finished up his sashimi and was angling for more by the time that Hannah had chosen her first item. She glanced over in Mother's direction and gave a big smile. Mother, who was too far away to intervene looked on helplessly as Hannah pulled off a tall parfait cup filled with chocolate sauce, pudding, cornflakes, and whipping cream, all topped off with a cherry. 'For dinner?' thought Mother to herself.

Mother chatted with Ikeda san. Everyone was enjoying their meal. It was delicious. Every now and then, she would glance over at the children. She felt a little out of control. Taro's plate pile was getting higher and higher and there was nothing she could do about it. He wolfed his food, washing it down with an endless supply of coca cola. Hannah, meanwhile, had only gotten through half of her parfait. She spent most of her time playing with Yuki kun, the baby.

After about half an hour everyone had finished. Mother smiled and bowed. "*Domo arigato gozaimashita*—thank you very much." The children followed suit. They bowed. "*Domo arigato*," they said to Ikeda san. When everyone got outside, Mother noticed that Taro was moving very slowly.

"I've got to go to the washroom," he said, moving slowly back towards the interior of the restaurant.

"We'll wait here," said Mother.

When Taro reappeared about ten minutes later, he was looking green in the face.

"I don't feel very well," he said.

'Oh dear,' thought Mother to herself. The last thing she needed was for Taro to throw up all over Ikeda san's car on the drive home.

≈≈≈

Taro sat down on the curb in the parking lot. Ikeda san noticed that things were amiss.

"*Daijoubu*? Are you okay, Taro," he asked.

"*Daijoubu*," replied Mother. "I think he ate too much."

"Yes," agreed Mr. Ikeda. He smiled. "Taro ate many, many plates," he said.

"Maybe, I can get him some stomach medicine," said Yuko, Ikeda san's daughter.

Just then, a loud *b-u-r-p* erupted. Taro sat up, and smiled. "There, I feel much better now," he said. "Dinner was delicious!"

Everyone laughed. Yuko and her family waved goodbye. Taro, Hannah, Mother and *Obaachan* got into Ikeda san's car and off they went. It was dark now and they drove mostly in silence. When they got home to their little house in Iwagijima, Mr. Ikeda got out of his car and opened his trunk. He handed Mother her bag of groceries.

"*Domo*," said Mother.

He reached back into the trunk. "Taro, Hannah chan, come here," he said.

He handed each of them two shopping bags. "*Dozo*," he said. "These are a few little treats from *Obaachan*."

"*Ehhhhh*," said Taro.

"*Arigato*," said Hannah.

Obaachan smiled and waved from the backseat.

CHAPTER 30

THE SECRET

"I don't want to go to school today, Mom," announced Hannah at the breakfast table.

"Oh," said Mother. "Do you get a test?" she asked.

"No, it's not that. I don't care about tests," said Hannah.

"Is it something that I can help you with?" asked Mother.

"No, I don't think so," said Hannah, her voice trailing off quietly. "It's just that, all of the girls are being kind of mean to me."

"What are they doing?" demanded Taro, always ready to protect his sister. "How are they being mean?" he asked.

"Well, it's just that they're always giggling and talking behind my back. If I ask what's so funny they just giggle more. They keep saying, *naisho, naisho*," said Hannah.

"*Naisho, naisho*, what does that mean, Hannah?" asked Mother.

"Well, it kind of means 'secret,' said Hannah.

"Oh, I see," said Mother. "So, they have a secret that they don't want to share with you."

"I don't know," said Hannah. "But it's kind of mean. When I walk near them they just stop talking. I feel kind of left out and embarrassed when they do that. Oh, never mind. It doesn't matter."

"Oh…just forget about them," said Taro. "If that happens to me I just ignore it."

"What if no one will play with me at break time any more?" asked Hannah.

"Hmmm" said Mother thinking. "I have an idea. Why don't you bring something in your pack that you like to do."

"Yaa, Hannah. Why don't you bring an Archie comic or a Calvin and Hobbes?" said Taro. "Whenever I bring those to school, all the kids want to look at them. They even want me to tell them what's going on," said Taro.

"That's a great idea, Hannah," said Mother.

"Yaa, I guess so," said Hannah.

"Or, how about bringing a drawing book or a journal or some writing paper. You could write a letter to your friends back in Canada," suggested Mother.

"Yaa, that's a good idea," said Hannah "I'll bring a comic and some paper."

"If you do that," said Mother, "you won't have anything to worry about. If they ask you to play with them you can leave everything where it is but if they are being secretive, then at least you'll have lots of things to do on your own."

"Yaa, I'll do that," said Hannah confidently. And if they do that stupid *naisho, naisho,* then I won't even care."

"Good thinking, Hannah!" cheered Taro.

"You guys had better hurry up, the kids'll be here soon," said Mother.

"Come on, Hannah, lets go!" said Taro, moving towards the entry hall.

"Oh, wait!" said Mother. "Here is a little something for you to get a treat on your way home from school."

She took out her wallet and handed each of the children two, one hundred yen coins.

THE SECRET

Mother gave Hannah a big hug.

"Oh boy, thanks Mom," said Taro.

"Thanks Mom, I love you," said Hannah.

∾∾

Mother put away the breakfast things and cleaned up the dishes. She did the laundry and was hanging it out to dry upstairs on the balcony.

"*Ohayo gozaimasu!*" yelled a woman from somewhere across the courtyard. Mother's eyes darted from house to house. She spotted the woman on a second floor balcony, her hands waving back and forth and her face peering out from between two pairs of men's trousers hanging on her clothes line.

"It's hot today, isn't it?" she said.

"Yes, very hot!" replied Mother.

"I am the second cousin of Mrs. Ikeda," she said. "How do you like Iwagi?"

"Iwagi is a very beautiful island," said Mother. "And the people here are very kind."

"*Domo, domo,*" replied the woman, bowing and smiling, exposing a front row of crooked teeth. "My niece has been to Canada. She has visited the Rocky Mountains. Canada is very beautiful."

Mother bowed. "*Domo, domo,*" she said.

Most people that Mother met were somehow related to Mr. or Mrs. Ikeda. The Ikeda family had been on the island for many generations. A good number of the people of Iwagijima seemed connected. Everyone, almost, knew that Mother, Father, Taro and Hannah were on Iwagi because of the efforts of Mr. and Mrs. Ikeda. They knew that the Ikeda's youngest daughter, Sachiko, who no longer lived on the island, had asked her parents to take care of this Canadian family. Sachiko had spent one year living with Mother, Father and the children in Vancouver, teaching Japanese to Taro and Hannah. When

Mother had mentioned to Sachiko one day that she would like to take Taro and Hannah to Japan, Sachiko had been eager to make arrangements. "My parents can help you get settled," she had said. Perhaps because of this connection, thought Mother, the people of Iwagi were very friendly and helpful.

Mother spent much of the rest of the day cleaning and tidying her small house. She remembered back to her first week on the island when she had discovered a *mukade*, a very large, very poisonous millipede crawling along the upper wall in the tatami room. Mother, not wanting to alarm the children, secretly took out the vacuum cleaner and tried to suck up the large insect. The millipede, stronger and faster than Mother's vacuum, slipped away into a crack in the ceiling, never to be seen again. And never to be mentioned, not even to Auntie Rhonda, Father's sister, who slept in the tatami room when she came all the way from Canada to visit Taro and Hannah.

Iwagi had been full of adventure and surprises, but their time here was fast coming to an end. In just two weeks, school would be finished for Taro and Hannah. And Mother, Father, and the children would be leaving the small island.

Mother looked at the boxes and buckets of seashells and pieces of broken pottery. She looked at Taro's prized collection of dead fighting beetles, lined up neatly along the shelf.

"I'm taking these home," he had said. "I'm going to give them to my friends."

Vacuuming was easy, thought Mother to herself. It's deciding what to pack that will be the problem.

Mother could hear voices in the lane. 'Is it that time already?' She looked at her watch. It was already two forty five. 'This must be one of their early days,' thought Mother.

THE SECRET

"Hi Mom," called out Taro. "Phew, it's hot today. I got a melon soda from the machine."

"Melon soda, that sounds interesting. Is it good?" asked Mother.

"It's delicious!" said Taro.

"Look what I got," said Hannah.

"Hannah got this dumb little plastic toy out of the machine instead of a drink," said Taro.

"It's not dumb!" retorted Hannah. "It's cute! Look Mom, see.... it's a puppy. It was only two hundred yen!"

"Yes, I see," said Mother. "Cute! How was school today?"

"It was so hot!" said Hannah. "We worked outside in the garden."

"Oh," said Mother. "That sounds like fun. What did you do, exactly, in the garden?" she asked.

"Well, my class is growing *satoimo*, that's sweet potato, and so we have to take care of the plants."

"So... you watered the plants?" asked Mother.

"No, I was number six. Numbers six, seven, and eight had to pull the weeds out. You see, Miyamoto sensei calls out different numbers to do different things. The number of my garden tool bag is six so I had to pull out weeds."

"Garden tools?" asked Mother.

"You know Mom, the tools you need to dig the dirt with, like the *kumanote*" said Hannah.

"The what?" asked Mother.

"The *kumanote*, you know, it has a claw to dig with," said Hannah.

Mother smiled. She thought that it was funny that Hannah knew the names of the tools in Japanese, but not in English.

"When everything is grown," continued Hannah, "we get to eat it."

"Yaa," said Taro. "We're going to make a big vegetable stew."

"What's your vegetable, Taro?" asked Hannah.

"We're growing carrots," he said. "But we did music class today, not gardening," said Taro. "I like music better. It's easy."

"Are you learning any new songs?" asked Mother.

"Well, we're doing a song with sign language," said Taro. "We sing the words and do the signs. It's so deaf people can understand too. Do you know how you say 'flower' in sign language, Mom?" asked Taro.

"No, I don't know any sign language," said Mother. "It must be hard!"

"No, look....flower is like this. It's easy Mom." Taro showed Mother how to make the sign for flower.

"Cool," said Hannah. "I hope that we get to learn it too."

"Did you use your Archie comic today, Hannah?" asked Mother.

"No, I didn't need to use it. We played tag. Even Miyamoto sensei played with us," said Hannah.

"Oh, Mom," called Taro.

"Yes," said Mother.

"Look," said Taro, holding out his upturned palm.

"What, Taro? What is that?" asked Hannah.

"It's a marble, a special one. Kenji gave it to me," said Taro. "He really likes marbles."

"Kenji?" asked Mother. "Isn't he the one who was the bully at school?"

"Yaa," said Taro, "but he's pretty nice to me now. We're friends.

CHAPTER 31

BIG FLUSH / SMALL FLUSH

Recently, Mother had noticed that often when she went into the toilet, the ends of the toilet paper roll had been folded into a neat triangle. She doubted that Father or Taro would have taken the time to do this. In fact, they probably wouldn't even notice it.

"Hannah, come here for a second, please," called out Mother to Hannah, who was drawing in the tatami mat room.

"Yes Mom, what is it?" asked Hannah.

"Oh, I just wanted to show you something," replied Mother.

"Where are you?" asked Hannah.

"I'm in the bathroom," replied Mother.

Hannah walked over to the bathroom. "Yes, Mom…"

"Look at the toilet paper," said Mother. "Did you do that?" she asked.

"Uh huh," replied Hannah. "Don't you know, Mom, that you're supposed to leave the toilet nice and neat for the next person. You always make triangles. Didn't you know that?" she asked.

"It's very nice," said Mother. "I've seen it done like that in fancy hotels."

"No…." said Hannah. "You're always supposed to do it."

"Oh," said Mother. "Where did you learn that?" she asked Hannah.

"At school. Everybody does it at school. I never used to do it but every time I used the toilet, it was like a triangle, so now I always do it. You should do it too, Mom," said Hannah. "In Japan you are supposed to."

"Yes," replied Mother. "It seems like a nice thing to do, I will," said Mother.

Hannah had become very interested in toilets and washrooms since coming to Japan. At the train station in Fukuyama, Hannah had pointed out to Mother the fact that there were two types of flushes.

"See, Mom," she had said. "That *kanji* means 'small,' so if you push the handle that way, only a little water comes out. Watch!" Hannah pushed the handle towards the character for 'small' and the toilet began to flush. When it had stopped flushing, she pointed to the character for 'big'. "And, if you push the handle this way, you get a big flush with lots of water," she explained to Mother. Hannah pushed the handle to 'big' and the toilet flushed once again.

"I see," said Mother. "That's interesting," she said. She wondered if anybody outside the stall was listening, or able to understand their conversation.

Hannah, over the course of her travels in Japan, had discovered many different kinds of toilets. She learned that, often, if you pushed a button somewhere, something interesting might happen.

"Mom," she yelled from a neighbouring stall in a department store washroom. "Push the button on the side wall."

Mother located the button in her cubicle and pushed it. Sounds of a waterfall flowed out from a small speaker on the wall.

"It's cool, isn't it," yelled Hannah above the water sounds.

On another occasion, this time in a small *monjayaki* restaurant in Tokyo, Hannah returned from the washroom in a very excited and agitated state.

"Taro, you've *got* to go to the bathroom. You won't believe it!"

BIG FLUSH / SMALL FLUSH

Taro got up from his seat and off he went. Hannah waited for his return. She sat on the edge of her seat craning her neck towards the hallway which led to the washroom. When Taro returned, she jumped up. The two children began laughing. Mother, who was just paying the bill, shooed them outside. "Get outside! You are too noisy. You are disturbing the other customers."

Once outside, Mother learned what all the commotion was about.

"It was amazing, Mom!" said Hannah. "When you flushed the toilet, these voices came out."

"Voices came out of the toilet?!" asked Mother. Both Taro and Hannah burst out laughing.

"I don't know where it came from," said Hannah. "But it was so funny. What did yours say, Taro? Mine started telling a story about a grandmother and a grandfather in the woods."

"Yaa," laughed Taro. "I think mine did too. It was some kind of old folk tale, I think."

"Coming from the toilet?!" asked Mother.

"Yaa," said Hannah. "Come on, Taro, let's try it again!"

Mother interrupted. "No, Hannah, I think you've had enough. We've got to get going anyway."

Perhaps Taro's and Hannah's most amusing toilet experience came while staying at a hotel in Kobe. Mother and the children had just checked in. Mother had pulled out a book and was about to sit down and relax when she heard a lot of laughter coming from the room's bathroom. She walked over and listened by the door.

"Just sit down, Taro. And push that button," directed Hannah.

The next thing that Mother heard was a yell from Taro and then a lot of giggling.

"Hey, what are you guys doing in there?" called out Mother while giving a loud knock on the locked door.

"Oh, nothing," replied Taro.

The two children erupted in laughter. When they finally came out of the bathroom they were both smiling.

"You should try the toilet seat," said Taro. "It's amazing!"

"Yaa," giggled Hannah. "It's warm and if you push these buttons, water shoots up your butt!"

"But you have to sit down first, Mom, before you push the buttons," said Taro.

Both children began laughing. "Yaa," said Hannah, otherwise you get sprayed in the face, right, Taro?"

"Shut up, Hannah!" said Taro.

CHAPTER 32

CATCHING DRAGONFLIES

These days, Mr. Ikeda dropped over to the house more frequently. Sometimes he would bring copies of photographs he had taken of Mother and the children on their outings in Iwagi.

"How many more days do you have on Iwagijima?" he asked Mother one day.

"We are leaving next Monday," replied Mother. "We have only this weekend and next weekend."

"*Ah so desuka*—I see," said Mr. Ikeda shaking his head slowly. "Too soon," he said.

"Yes, the time has gone by very quickly," remarked Mother.

"I will come tomorrow morning at nine o'clock, before it gets too hot," he said. "I have some place special to show Taro kun and Hannah chan."

~·~

Mother got the children to bed earlier that night. "Tomorrow, after breakfast, Ikeda san is coming to take us out," explained Mother.

"But I wanted to sleep in tomorrow," said Taro.

"You can," replied Mother. "Normally you get up at six forty five, but tomorrow you get to sleep in until eight thirty!"

The children, being tired from their week at school, went to bed without much of a fuss. Mother stayed up. She tidied the kitchen and the tatami mat room and then sat down to relax with a cup of tea.

※

The next morning, a few minutes before nine o'clock, the doorbell rang. 'Ping pong.' "Can you get that, Hannah," asked Mother. "It will be Ikeda san." Hannah opened the door in the *genkan*.

"*Ohayo*," she said.

"*Ohayo*, Hannah chan," said Mr. Ikeda.

Taro came out of the washroom. "*Ohayo*, Taro kun."

"*Ohayo*," replied Taro. "Where are we going today?" he asked.

"We are going to catch dragonflies. Have you ever caught dragonflies before, Taro kun?" asked Mr. Ikeda.

"No, not really," replied Taro. "How do we do it?"

"Come on. I'll show you."

Mother and Taro and Hannah followed Ikeda san up the lane to where his truck was parked. They squeezed into the cab. About half way around the island road Mr. Ikeda turned down a narrow dirt path and parked. Everyone jumped out of the truck. Mr. Ikeda reached into the back and pulled out a long pole with a net on one end. "Hold this please," he said to Taro. He reached in again, this time grabbing a clear plastic bug catching box. He handed this to Hannah. Ikeda san moved down a slope to the stream. The children followed after him.

"Ouch, careful Taro!" yelled Hannah. "Be careful with that pole."

Taro was swinging the pole as if it were a long wooden sword. "Hiyaahh!" he yelled, swishing the pole from side to side as if protecting himself from the enemy. Ikeda san, putting his hand to his mouth, motioned for the children to be quiet and listen.

"Look, can you see the dragonflies?" he asked.

CATCHING DRAGONFLIES

The children stopped and watched. "Wow...." said Taro. "There are *tons* of dragonflies here!"

Ikeda san smiled.

"Taro, look at that red one!" said Hannah. "It looks like a light."

"Cool!" replied Taro. "I'm going to catch it," he said. "Look out!" He whipped the pole quickly through the air."

"You're way too slow," said Hannah. "Let me try! I can get one!"

After a few more whips to the sky, Taro handed the pole to Hannah.

"You've got to flip the net, Hannah—*not* like that—just flip it!"

"I can do it, Taro. Leave me alone," said Hannah.

"There's one—an electric blue one," said Taro. "Let *me* get it."

"No, I can get it!!" said Hannah. Hannah swung the long pole in the air. She did not manage to catch the dragonfly. Hannah tried several more times and then handed the pole back to Taro. "It's too heavy," she said.

Taro took the pole and began thrashing it about in the air. Ikeda san, standing a few metres down stream, watched the children. He smiled.

"It's quite difficult," he said. "Shall I try?"

Taro walked over to Mr. Ikeda and handed him the pole. Both children watched. Mr. Ikeda lifted the pole. With a graceful half turn, he swished the net through the air; a quick flick of his wrist and he had neatly trapped a large electric blue dragonfly.

"*Atta, atta*!" yelled Taro and Hannah together. "You've got one. You've got one!"

Mr. Ikeda carefully lowered the pole to the ground. He gently took the dragonfly in his fingers and then lifted the net. "Hannah chan," he called. "Open up your box." Hannah ran over quickly and slowly slid open the top of the bug catcher. Ikeda san released the dragonfly.

"Look, Taro, it's in my box," said Hannah.

Taro's eyes darted along the stream. "There's another one. A red one! Ikeda san, can you catch that one?" he asked.

Mr. Ikeda raised the long pole into the air. He stopped and didn't move. Suddenly, the net, like a bird of prey swooped down on top of the red dragonfly.

"Yay, another one!" yelled Hannah.

"Taro kun, come here," said Ikeda san. "You take out the dragonfly." Taro, reached into the net. With the thumb and forefinger of his right hand he grabbed the dragonfly. The dragonfly started to thrash about. Slowly and gently Taro lifted the net with his other hand. "Ouch, ouch. Hurry up Hannah. Open the box. It's biting me," he yelled, dancing around the pole.

"I can't. The other one will get out!" replied Hannah.

"Hurry up!" snapped Taro. "I can't hold on to it any longer!"

Hannah shook the blue dragonfly to the bottom of the box and carefully slid the top open. Taro released his fingers from the insect and tried to flick it into the box. "It won't let go of me!" he yelled. "Ouch." He gave his hand a few violent shakes. Finally the dragonfly dropped into the bug catching box. "Ow, that hurt," said Taro.

Meanwhile, Ikeda san's net was up again and trolling the stream. Hannah admired the two dragonflies in her box. Taro carefully watched Ikeda san's hovering net. He saw the dragonfly and then the flash of the net as Mr. Ikeda whipped his pole through the air. In a single sweep he had trapped another dragonfly.

"Get it, Taro," called Hannah. "I'll open the box."

"No, Hannah. I'm not taking it out of the net. It bites! You get it. It's your turn!"

Ikeda san, who saw the children quarrelling, called them over. "Taro kun, Hannah chan, come here. I will show you how to carry the dragonfly."

Taro and Hannah walked over to the net and crouched down. Ikeda san lifted the net carefully with one hand. He slipped the middle and forefinger of his other hand between the body of the insect and its wings. He lifted it gently.

"If you pick it up like this, it can't pinch you. See?" he said. He held his arm out for the children to see. "Taro kun, you try." Mr. Ikeda guided Taro's hand. "Open these two fingers. Slowly, that's it." Ikeda san transferred the dragonfly from his hand to Taro's. "See?" he said. The legs of the dragonfly were flailing about but because of the positioning of Taro's fingers, they were unable to latch on to him, to pinch him.

"*Iii ne*—that's cool!" said Taro.

"Let me try, I want to try," said Hannah

"Put your hand out," instructed Taro. "Closer. Now, open these two fingers. You've got to move in closer," said Taro.

Hannah took a tentative step towards Taro and the writhing dragonfly. Taro put the insect between her fingers. "See, Hannah, you can do it!" said Taro.

"*Dekita ne*—you did it!" said Ikeda san, who had been watching the two children from a few feet away.

"Open the box, Taro," said Hannah. "I want to put it in. Hurry! Open it up!"

"Okay, okay," said Taro, sliding open the lid. "Put it in. Hurry, before the other ones get away."

Hannah quickly released the dragonfly into the box. Taro slid the lid shut.

"Come on," said Mr. Ikeda. "I will teach you how to catch them."

For the next hour, Taro and Hannah each took turns catching dragonflies. The small plastic bug catching box was brimming and buzzing with insects.

"I'm getting hot," said Mr. Ikeda. "Shall we go and get a drink?"

"Yaa, I'm thirsty," said Hannah.

"Me too," said Taro.

Mr. Ikeda led the children across the field to his brother-in-law's house. He smiled at Mother. "He is a bachelor. He is very messy, but don't mind. We can have a drink here."

Everyone followed Ikeda san through the courtyard and into the old house. It was indeed very messy. Boxes were piled everywhere. Mr. Ikeda pushed them to the side to create a narrow path.

"You can wash your hands here," he said, pointing to a sink. He searched through some of the cartons and boxes and pulled out some paper towels. "Let's sit in here," he said, leading the children to a small room, which was even more jumbled than the hallway. He clicked on the air conditioner and then the wide screen T.V. He pushed magazines and books off onto the floor, clearing a place on the sofa for Mother and the children to sit down. "*Dozo*—please sit down," he said and promptly left the room.

Taro and Hannah sat down giggling. "Whoah, Mom ... what is all this junk?" asked Taro.

"It's amazing," said Hannah. "So much stuff! Who lives here anyways?"

Ikeda san returned with several cans of soda and some ice cream bars. He handed some to Mother and Taro and Hannah and took a soda and an ice cream for himself.

"*Arigato*—thank you," said the children.

"*Domo*," said Mother.

Ikeda san began scavenging about, looking here and there under stacks of paper and inside boxes. Finally, he pulled out a remote control and handed it to Taro. "*Dozo*," he said.

Taro flipped through the channels, stopping now and then to watch cartoons or game shows. Ikeda san picked up and began sorting through a pile of glossy magazines. When he came across ones with comics or interesting pictures he handed them over to Hannah or Taro. "You can keep these," he said.

CATCHING DRAGONFLIES

After everyone had finished their sodas and ice cream Mr. Ikeda stood up. "*Ikooka*—shall we go?"

"*Hai*—yes," responded Taro and Hannah.

Mother, Taro and Hannah followed behind Ikeda san in single file, being careful not to trip over the debris. Mr. Ikeda pulled things out from various boxes along the way. "Here, Hannah chan," he said, handing her an unopened box of chocolate cookies. "Taro kun, *dozo*," he said, passing Taro a package of rice crackers.

"*Arigato*," said the children, giggling.

Ikeda san pulled out a six pack of toilet paper rolls and smiled at Mother. "*Dozo*," he said, handing them to her.

Mother, who was a little embarrassed, smiled back. "*Domo*," she replied.

Outside, the children picked up the bug box and the long pole. They handed Mother their cookies and crackers and began walking back towards Ikeda san's truck. Everyone was tired.

When finally they arrived at the lane near their house, Mother and Taro and Hannah got out and thanked Mr. Ikeda.

"It was lots of fun," said Hannah.

"*Unh*," agreed Taro. "*Arigato*."

Mr. Ikeda smiled and waved good bye. Mother and the children walked down the lane to their small house.

"What should we do with the dragonflies," asked Hannah.

"I know," said Taro. "Let's open the box and let them fly away."

"Good idea!" said Hannah.

The two children pried the lid off of the box. One by one the dragonflies flew up and away. "Oh, oh, there's one still left inside," said Hannah. "Its wing is broken. What should we do Taro?"

"I know," said Taro. "Let's feed it to the cats."

CHAPTER 33

THE GOOD BYE SPEECH

Hannah had been working for several days now on a special homework assignment. "I don't know what else to write, Mom," she said. "How long do you think it should be?"

"Hmmm, I'm not sure," responded Mother. "Did Nakamoto sensei give you any ideas?"

"No, not really. She just said to write a *wakare no aisatsu*—a kind of good bye speech. She said to talk about my experiences at Iwagi Shogakko."

"So… she said you could talk about anything you wanted to?" asked Mother.

"Uh huh. Things like, well, things that are different between school here and school in Canada or….things that I learned or…. about things that I liked or didn't like. Stuff like that," replied Hannah.

"Well, that shouldn't be too hard," said Mother. "Did you talk about the new friends you made, or about Miyamoto sensei? He was pretty funny, wasn't he?" said Mother.

"Yaa," said Hannah. "He was fun, a little different than my teachers in Vancouver."

"What about some things that are different from Canada—like *kyuushoku*—school lunch, or wearing uniforms," suggested Mother.

"Yaa, Hannah," said Taro. "I talked about all the good food I got at lunch. I said that *kyuushoku* was my favourite thing about school."

"How about the toilets—how different they are, and how you didn't like them at first," said Mother.

"*MOM*! yelled Hannah. "I *can't* do that! That's *embarrassing*!"

"Well, how about the slippers and shoes. You know, always having to wear the right shoes to the right place. In Canada you only have to worry about one pair, right?"

"Yaa," said Hannah. I guess I could say how at first I couldn't walk in the slippers, how they always fell off. But now I can. I'll put that."

Hannah started to write. Mother was very surprised that Hannah's and Taro's worries were more about trying to figure out *what* to say rather than *how* to write it in Japanese. Mother was pleased.

"So, when do you have to present it?" asked Mother.

"Friday," said Taro. "We have to do it on Friday in front of the whole school in the assembly hall. What if I forget what to say," said Taro, fidgeting with his pencil.

"Yaa well, what if I make a bunch of mistakes," said Hannah.

"You guys will do fine. You can practice in front of me first," said Mother.

"Yaa, well *you* won't laugh. What if everybody laughs at us," said Hannah.

"They're not going to laugh at you," responded Mother. "Besides, it's a pretty amazing thing, don't you think? Doing it in Japanese," said Mother. "Imagine if *they* had to do it in English?"

"Yaa, I guess you're right. It'd be pretty hard for them to do it in English."

"You'll both do fine. And just think, after that, after this Friday, you're finished with school!"

"Hurray!" yelled Taro.

THE GOOD BYE SPEECH

"Yay!" yelled Hannah. "And we get the party after, too, on Saturday.

"You're having a party?" asked Mother.

"Oh yaa, Mom. I forgot to tell you. Remember when the girls in my class wouldn't talk to me and they were all giggly and everything?" asked Hannah. "You remember?! *Naisho, naisho,*" explained Hannah.

"Oh," said Mother. "The big secret! I remember now. So..?"

"So, Mom, the big secret was this party. They didn't want me to know that they were planning a party for me and Taro. You know, before we go back to Canada," said Hannah.

"Ah yes—*naisho, naisho,*" replied Mother.

Doing homework in the tatami mat room

CHAPTER 34

LAST DAY OF SCHOOL

The last day of school for Taro and Hannah had arrived. Mother had been invited to Iwagi Shogakko in the afternoon.

"Please come at two o'clock," directed Nakamoto sensei, the principal. "We will have an assembly. Two o'clock, *ne*?"

"*Domo, domo,*" replied Mother.

"Ah, time has been very short in Iwagi. It is already time for you to go. Too short!" repeated Nakamoto sensei. "Taro kun and Hannah chan have done very well, very well. In the beginning they made many mistakes, but now they understand about school in Iwagi very well. And also, they have made friends, many friends. It has been a good experience!" said Nakamoto sensei.

"*Domo, domo,*" replied Mother, bowing deeply in front of the principal.

৩৯

Many parents and younger siblings and grandmothers and grandfathers arrived at Iwagi Shogakko just before two p.m. They gathered in small groups in the shade under the leafy green trees in the playground. Some of the women fanned themselves with ornate Japanese fans. It was another very hot and humid day.

HANNAH CHAN

Nakamoto sensei greeted the parents and directed them into the auditorium. "*Dozo*," she said. "Please take your seats."

The school children buzzed with energy. They chattered away in rows near the front of the hall. Nakamoto sensei climbed up the stairs to the stage. She was a small, sturdy, confident woman with graying hair and sensible shoes. She adjusted the microphone. She welcomed her guests and the assembly began.

The first graders filed up onto the stage. There were only eight pupils in grade one, seven boys and one girl. The children recited their verses, each one, in turn, standing forward to hold up their *hiragana*—letter. There must have been a joke at the end, thought Mother, for everyone in the audience laughed. Mother laughed too, though she wasn't quite sure what had been funny. With a round of applause the first graders left the stage in a single file and went back to their seats.

Each grade, in turn, came up onto the stage. They sang or danced or acted out little skits. The visitors applauded. When all the grades had finished their performances and returned to their seats, Nakamoto sensei came back onto the stage and took hold of the microphone. She waited for everyone's attention. She cleared her throat and began:

"Today, is a very special day," she said. "It is the last day of school for Taro kun and Hannah chan. As you all know, Taro kun and Hannah chan have come to Iwagi Shogakko from Canada." She went on to describe the first time she had met them and how she had wondered and worried about how they would manage at Iwagi Shogakko. She said that both children had done very well, that they had learned a great deal. She continued by saying that not only had Taro kun and Hannah chan learned many things but also that the whole school at Iwagi Shogakko had learned from Taro and Hannah. They had learned about another country and culture and best of all, she said,

LAST DAY OF SCHOOL

they had all made new friendships. She bowed and thanked Taro kun and Hannah chan. The assembly hall applauded.

Mother felt a single tear trickle down her cheek. She wiped it away. People in the auditorium were straining to find Taro kun and Hannah chan among the children seated at the front. Some stole furtive glances at Mother while others looked directly at her, smiling and bowing. "*Domo, domo,*" they said softly. Mother bowed her head and smiled too. When the applause had faded, Nakamoto sensei called Taro up to the stage.

Mother's heart beat faster and her stomach tensed. Taro took the microphone from Nakamoto sensei's hand. Holding the microphone in one hand and his speech in the other, he began tentatively.

"My name is Taro Margolis. Thank you for listening to me," he said. Taro read his speech, frequently looking up at the audience. And gaining confidence as he went along, he spoke about things he had learned at Iwagi Shogakko. He talked about some differences between Canadian and Japanese schools. Finally, he talked about what he liked the most at school in Iwagi.

"My best class," he said, "is *kyuushoku*—lunch!" Everyone laughed. "I really liked lunch! In Canada we have to bring our own lunches every day. Most kids bring sandwiches. It is so boring! In Iwagi, I get to eat many things I like. Fish!" he said, "all kinds of fish. And squid and chicken, and beef!" The assembly hall once again burst out in laughter. "I loved lunch at Iwagi Shogakko. Thank you." He bowed deeply and handed the microphone back to Nakamoto sensei. Everyone clapped. Taro took his seat. Nakamoto sensei thanked Taro and then called Hannah chan to the stage.

Hannah sprung up from the edge of her seat. Her shoulders were tensed and bent forward. She walked quickly, unevenly, stumbling now and again as she made her way up to the stage. She took the microphone from Nakamoto sensei's hand. Her eyes darted through the audience and then looked down at the speech she was holding.

"Hello, everyone," she said in a small, nervous voice. "I am Hannah Margolis. Thank you for listening to me. Going to school in Japan is very different than going to school in Canada. At Iwagi Shogakko I got to do many fun things. I got to study about crabs at the beach. I got to have swimming lessons. I got to visit the old people at the old folks home. I even got to pick lemons and make lemonade. That was fun. Especially, riding, our whole class, in Miyamoto sensei's car. I liked to learn Japanese songs in music class. My favorite class of all, though, was English, 'cause it was soooo easy," said Hannah, losing her nervousness. Everyone in the auditorium laughed and clapped. Hannah continued more confidently now. She held her head up straight and pushed her shoulders back.

"Some things, though, were much harder for me here than in Canada," she said. "There were so many shoes and slippers to put on and take off all of the time. In Canada, it's easy. We only use one pair. Another thing which was hard, was getting changed in the classroom in front of all the boys; I didn't like that! Also, the toilets. They are different than the kind we use at school in Canada. At first, I wouldn't use them so my Mom said she would pay me one hundred yen each time I used the toilets. Because of that, I soon learned how to use them very well." The people in the audience laughed again. "I have had a good time at Iwagi Shogakko. All my teachers were so kind and I have made many new friends here. If anyone at Iwagi Shogakko has the chance, please come to visit me in Canada. *Arigato gozaimashita* " Hannah gave a deep bow. Everyone cheered and clapped. Hannah, now with a bounce in her step, moved off of the stage and returned to her seat.

Mother beamed. She was very proud of Taro kun and Hannah chan that afternoon.

CHAPTER 35

NEON LIGHTS

Mother and Father were busy sweeping and cleaning the small Japanese house. There was only one day left before their departure from Iwagijima.

"What are we going to do with all of those," asked Father, pointing to the boxes overflowing with potatoes and onions and shrivelled, molding citrus fruits."

"Hmm," said Mother. "Well, I don't think anyone else will want them." She stopped sweeping and thought for a second. "Let's just dump them out. We could take them up to the top of the hill and dump them. Nobody goes up there."

"Yes, I guess we could do that," said Father. "We'll just make sure no one is watching us when we do it."

"Watching what?" asked Hannah coming down the stairs, catching only the last bit of the conversation.

"Oh, never mind," said Father. "Are you and Taro almost ready for your party tonight? We'll have to go soon. Ikeuchi sensei is picking us up in about fifteen minutes."

"I'm ready," said Taro.

"I can hardly wait," said Hannah. "We get to swim in the ocean today. Finally, it's swimming season!"

"Yaa, *you* get to," said Taro. "But *I* don't. I can't even go in the water!" he said. "Why can't I go in, Mom? I'll be okay," pleaded Taro.

The doctor said that you shouldn't go swimming. He said you need to keep your knee out of the water for a few days. But it will be better soon, Taro," said Mother.

"It'll never get better. Stupid knee!" said Taro.

"You could put your feet in the water," said Mother.

"That's not fun! Everyone will be swimming and playing in the water except me. And this is supposed to be *my* farewell party!" said Taro.

"I know," said Mother softly. "It isn't fair is it. I'm sorry Taro. I wish there was something I could do."

༺♥༻

Soon there was a knock at the door. Mother, Father, Taro and Hannah squeezed into Ikeuchi sensei's car and they made their way across the island to a white, sandy beach. Already, many children were running in and out of the water, splashing and laughing. Taro put his head down.

"Come on Taro," said Hannah. "Let's build something."

"Nah….. I don't want to," said Taro, sitting down on the stairs.

"He'll be alright," whispered Father to Hannah. "Just leave him for a minute."

Mother started to chat with some of the parents. Father and Hannah wandered down the beach looking for shells. Taro remained seated, slowly swirling a small twig in the sand.

"Is he alright?" asked Kentaro's father.

Mother told him about Taro's knee injury and explained that he was feeling a little sad about not being able to go into the water.

"Oh, I see," said Kentaro's father. "That's unfortunate."

NEON LIGHTS

Mother strolled down the beach to find Hannah and Father. She found them, at the opposite end, poking at a large jellyfish with a stick.

"I'm getting hungry," said Hannah.

"I saw the parents and teachers setting up hibachis and unloading a lot of food from their cars," said Mother.

"Well, at least *that* should make Taro happy," said Hannah.

Just then, Mother noticed a wooden boat, a few yards away. The man that Mother had been talking to earlier was now maneuvering the boat close to the shore.

"Taro kun!" yelled Kentaro's father. "Please help me. I need help with my boat."

Taro looked up.

"Taro, please come!" yelled the man.

"*Hai,*" yelled Taro back. "I'm coming." He got up, shook the sand from his shorts and began running over in the direction of the boat.

"Climb in," said the man, extending his arm to Taro. Taro climbed into the boat and the two of them headed back out into the water.

Soon, a group of boys from Taro's class swam over to them. "Can we come. Can we come?" they yelled. Kentaro's father motioned for them to climb aboard. As the boat moved away from the shore and into the deeper waters, Mother could see the man showing Taro how to paddle and steer the boat using a long wooden pole at the back. By pushing the pole back and forth and back and forth, the boat was propelled through the water. Mother could see that Taro was smiling now, steering the boat and chatting away with the other boys.

The smell of grilled meat filled the air. "Let's eat!" said Hannah. "It must be ready by now."

"Hannah chan, *dozo,*" called out one of the mothers, passing Hannah a couple of '*onigiri*—rice balls' and a bowl containing dipping sauce. Hannah ate up the rice balls and then filled her bowl with barbequed beef and grilled vegetables.

"Mmm, this is good!" she said to Mother. "*Oishii*—delicious!" she said to the other parents.

Soon the boatload of boys pulled up to the shore. They all jumped out, including Taro, and ran up to the barbeque area. Mother walked down to Kentaro's father who was just pulling the boat up onto the sand. "*Domo arigato*," she said bowing deeply. There was not a trace of sadness on Taro's face as he, along with the other children, filled their bowls.

"Wow, Mom, did you see?" said Taro through a mouthful of food. "There's beef and chicken and fish and prawns."

"I know," said Mother. "It's better than hamburgers and hot dogs, isn't it? Make sure you save some for the others."

"Alright," said Taro, walking over to one of the hibachis and holding out his bowl for more. "I will."

For the rest of the evening, Taro and Hannah and the other children dug pits and tunnels and built giant, elaborate mountains out of the fine sand. They worked in teams, each team trying to outdo the other. Teachers wandered from group to group taking photographs.

The children joined in games. Hannah's favorite game was: 'smash the watermelon.' When it was Hannah's turn, a teacher tied on a blindfold and twirled her around and around. He handed her a wooden bat. Hannah whacked the sand over and over with the bat trying to hit the melon.

"It's over here, to your right."

"One step back. No, to your left" yelled the children, laughing and giving her misguided directions. "It's because of your bad Japanese," chortled the boys, when Hannah, unsuccessful in her attempt, removed her blindfold.

"That's not fair!" she yelled back. "You were tricking me!"

NEON LIGHTS

❦

As the sunlight faded and the parents finished packing up their cars, the teachers gathered the children around in a circle.

"We hope everyone had a good time tonight," said Ikeuchi sensei. "It has been a happy time to have Taro and Hannah at Iwagi Shogakko. Tomorrow, they will be leaving our island. We would like to sing a farewell song for Taro and Hannah."

Taro and Hannah, unsure of what they should do, smiled embarrassedly and looked down at their feet in the sand. In gentle voices the children began to sing. A tear fell down Mother's cheek. She wiped it away. 'Everyone had been so kind,' she thought. When the song ended, Mother and Father, Taro and Hannah bowed. "*Domo arigato*," they said softly.

The children dispersed, rushing off to find their wet things. Swimsuits and sandals and sandy towels were strewn around the beach. One by one they gathered up their belongings and came up to Taro and Hannah to say their goodbyes. "*Sayonara*," they said. "*Mata kite, ne*—please come back and visit us." Gradually, the beach became quiet. It was a beautiful, moonlit evening. The sea was calm and flat. Only a small group of children remained playing at the water's edge.

"Taro kun, Hannah chan, '*kite*—come here,'" yelled one of the boys. Taro and Hannah walked down to the water.

"*Mite*—watch!" said Satoru kun. He picked up a handful of wet sand and threw it out across the water.

"*Eh*! That's amazing!" said Taro.

"How did you do that?" asked Hannah.

Satoru picked up another handful and tossed it into the ocean. "You try it!" he said.

Taro and Hannah each bent down and picked up some wet sand. They flung it over the water.

"Cool!" said Hannah, completely mesmerized. She scooped up another handful and threw it in. "*M...o...m*, come here!" yelled Hannah. "You've *got* to see this Mom, hurry!"

Mother walked down to where the children were standing. "What is it?" she asked.

"Watch this!" said Taro, picking up another handful of sand. "Watch!!"

Mother watched as Taro and Hannah threw the sand out across the water. The ocean sprang alive as the sand particles hit its surface. Hundreds and hundreds of tiny lights flitted for just a few seconds before falling into the darkness.

"Wow!" said Mother. "I've never seen anything like it." She stooped down, scooped up some wet sand and skimmed it across the phosphorescent sea.

"How does it do that?" asked Taro.

"I don't know," said Mother.

"It's like neon lights on the water," said Hannah.

Taro propelling the boat

NEON LIGHTS

Hannah playing 'Suikawari' or 'Smash the Watermelon.'

Making tunnels at the beach

CHAPTER 36

SAYONARA, IKEDASAN

Father helped Mr. Ikeda load the three heavy suitcases into the back of his pick-up truck. They would be kept in a safe place for about two weeks. Later, the suitcases would be sent by 'Black Cat' courier to the airport in Tokyo, just in time for the final flight back to Canada.

"We'll be back in a few minutes," said Mother to the children. "We just have to help Mr. Ikeda with our bags."

Mother and Father squeezed into the cab and off they went. Mother was surprised when Mr. Ikeda came to a stop, not at his house, but at the Co-op Hardware store in the centre of town. Mr. Ikeda got out and started unloading the suitcases. Father helped him.

"We'll leave these here," said Mr. Ikeda, placing the bags outside, on the concrete, just behind the store. He smiled and began walking back towards the truck.

Father looked at Mother in alarm. "But my computer is in there," he said to Mother. "And look, the suitcases are in full view, only a few steps from the main street. I don't think this is right. Does Ikeda san know that I have a computer in there? You'd better ask him," said Father.

Mother, with her limited Japanese, was always called upon to solve the family's problems.

"Okay, I'll ask," she said reluctantly.

"Ikeda san, *koko de ii desuka*?—Is it alright to leave them here?" asked Mother. "There is a computer inside. Is it safe?"

Mr. Ikeda looked over at Mother. He seemed confused.

"The suitcases," said Mother again. "Is it safe to leave them here, outside, for two weeks?"

"Oh, the suitcases!" said Mr. Ikeda. "Yes, yes, of course it is safe," he said smiling. "It is safe to leave them out here."

Father shrugged at Mother.

"*Domo, domo*," he said, bowing.

On the way back home, Mother asked Mr. Ikeda to please stop in front of the vending machines. Father jumped out of the truck. He plugged in some coins and retrieved four large cans of cold beer. When they arrived at home he held up the cans to Mr. Ikeda, smiling.

"*Bieru*?" he offered.

"*Ah, domo, domo*," said Mr. Ikeda.

Once inside, Father and Mr. Ikeda sat down at the low table in the tatami mat room. Father filled Mr. Ikeda's glass with beer. Mr. Ikeda picked up the can and filled Father's glass. Mother brought in some rice crackers, placed them on the table, and sat down. She held out her glass for Mr. Ikeda to fill.

"*Compai*—Cheers!" said Mother, Father and Mr. Ikeda, clinking their glasses together.

"Tomorrow you leave Iwagijima. Too bad. Too bad! You must stay longer next time," said Mr. Ikeda.

Mother, Father and Mr. Ikeda, laughed and chatted and refilled their glasses with beer. Mother felt happy and relaxed. 'It is funny,' she thought to herself. 'But this is the very first time that I have been able to understand Mr. Ikeda—to really talk to him'.

After about an hour had passed, Ikeda san got up from the table.

SAYONARA, IKEDASAN

"*Jaa,* it is getting late. I am sure that you still have many things left to do," he said.

Mr. Ikeda said good bye to Mother and Father. He called for the children to come down from upstairs.

"Good bye," he said to Taro and Hannah, his eyes welling up with tears. "Please come back again, *ne*."

Taro and Hannah bowed deeply. "*Arigato. Arigato. Domo arigato,*" they said together.

Mother wiped away a tear that had run down her cheek. This had been happening a lot these last few days. She looked over at the children and then at Mr. Ikeda. He had been more than a mentor, more than a teacher. Had the children had a grandfather on Iwagijima, it would have been Ikeda san. Mr. Ikeda bowed and slowly backed out of the entry hall. Mother, Father, Taro and Hannah bowed too. "*Sayonara,*" they said waving, as Ikeda san got into his truck and pulled away.

Ikeda san and Mother

CHAPTER 37

LEAVING IWAGIJIMA

The final cleaning and packing happened once the children had gone to bed. It was much easier for Mother to make decisions about what to keep and what to throw away when Hannah was not peering over her shoulder.

"What! …. You're throwing this away?!" asked Hannah, holding up a large, pink scallop shell. "You can't throw away that. I need it," she said, continuing to rummage through the 'discard pile'. "Mom! I'm taking this with me!"

Mother was getting nowhere. The more things she threw away, the more things Hannah retrieved and placed in her own, 'to keep' pile.

"It's getting late, Hannah," said Mother. "You've got to go to bed."

"But, I want to help," said Hannah. "I want to make sure that you keep the things I need," she said.

"Yes, of course I will," said Mother wearily. "I will keep everything you need."

"You promise?" asked Hannah.

"Yes, I promise. Now off to bed," pleaded Mother.

Once Hannah and Taro had gone upstairs, Father opened the fridge and took out the last of the cans of beer he had bought from the vending machine. "Want some?" he asked Mother.

"Sure," said Mother with a sigh. "Let's take a break."

Mother and Father sat down in the tatami mat room. It was cool and quiet. All that could be heard was the buzz of the air conditioner and sometimes, above that, the rythmic chanting of the elderly woman next door. Every now and then the hum of her deep voice was punctuated by the clap of her hands or the ringing of a bell. Mother was familiar with these sounds. When Father was away in Canada and she lay alone at night with the children in the darkness, she found these sounds comforting. The assurance that someone was nearby praying made her feel safe in this very foreign place.

"So… we're getting there," said Father. Everything is almost done. The suitcases have been sent. The place looks pretty clean, don't you think?"

"Yaa, I guess so," said Mother. "All we have to do is get rid of all *this* junk," she said, pointing to the loose papers and notebooks, the old toys and the collection of bottle caps. "And there's the fridge… What do we do with all of the food? The pickles that Furumura san gave us. And the fish and the rice balls; we can't finish it all."

"We'll just have to throw it away," said Father.

"Yes, but raw garbage doesn't go out until Thursday," said Mother. "And all the other stuff isn't supposed to go out until next week."

"Ah…don't worry about it," said Father. "We can just put it altogether in one big bag and Mr. Ikeda can take it out on Thursday for us."

"No, we can't do that," said Mother. "It's not right. You can't mix paper and plastic and food altogether. It's got to be separated. No, nobody does that."

"Well, there's nothing much else we can do now," said Father. "We're leaving tomorrow morning. It's not that big of a deal. I'm sure that *they* even do it sometimes."

LEAVING IWAGIJIMA

"Oh, I don't know," said Mother. "I don't feel right about doing that." Mother sighed. "Well, I guess it *is* only once. We don't really have much of a choice, do we? I'm getting tired," she said.

Before they went up to bed, everything was neat and tidy and in its place.

※

The next morning, the children were up early and buzzing with excitement.

"When are we going?" asked Taro.

"We'll take the ten o'clock ferry," said Father. "But we'll have to leave before then."

"Mrs. Furumura is coming by about nine fifteen, to help us with our bags," said Mother.

Taro and Hannah went outside. Taro sat down on the front stoop to play his Gameboy. Hannah bounced a ball off the stone wall across from the house. Mother and Father gathered up all the belongings and set them down outside the door.

Soon Mrs. Furumura arrived, pulling a cart.

"*Ohayo Gozaimasu,*" she said.

"*Ohayo,*" said the children.

"Please put your bags in here," said Mrs. Furumura.

A few minutes later, Mr. Furumura came driving up the lane in his little red car.

"*Dozo,*" he said, motioning for Mother and the children to get in. "I will give you a ride," he said.

Father took hold of the cart of luggage and he and Mrs. Furumura began walking towards the port. Mother smiled. Mrs. Furumura spoke no English. From the back window of the car Mother could see Mrs. Furumura chatting away. Father was bowing and saying, '*domo, domo,*' as he walked along beside her.

At the port, a small group of people had gathered around. Mrs. Ikeda, dressed in her blue Co-op Hardware store apron, joined the group.

"What's that you have, Taro," asked Mr. Furumura, looking at the box Taro held in his hand.

"It's a *nokogiri*," said Taro, proudly holding up the fighting beetle for everyone to see. "It's a present for my friend Take, in Nagoya. We're going there to visit him. It's a present from Iwagijima," he said.

"That's a big one!" said Mr. Furumura. "I'm sure he will like that. They don't have big ones like that in Nagoya," he said. Everyone in the group smiled and laughed.

Mrs. Ikeda stepped forward. "So…. what should we do with the left over garbage?" she asked. Before Mother could answer, Mrs. Furumura spoke up.

"Don't worry….." she said. "I will take care of it. I will take all of the raw garbage up to my *hatake* tomorrow and spread it out. Don't worry. I will take care of it. It will be good for the garden."

Mother's heart quickened and she felt her face turning red. "Oh no, please don't trouble yourself," she said. "Mr. Ikeda will take it. He'll take it out on Thursday."

"No, no. Don't worry," replied Mrs. Furumura. "I will do it. It is really no bother at all and those cats……we can't leave it unattended until Thursday."

Mother panicked. She couldn't have Mrs. Furumura empty her garbage. What a disaster, she thought. She could just see old Mr. and Mrs. Furumura hauling the big bag up to their *hatake*. What a surprise they'd get when they spread it all out. 'Oh no,' thought Mother. 'It wouldn't work. I can't let it happen.'

"But, but, Mr. Ikeda will take it out," said Mother, looking helplessly towards Mrs. Ikeda for help. Mother had not only cheated on the garbage by filling one bag with all kinds of different things, things that were meant to be sorted, things like plastic and paper and pickles, all mixed together in one great jumble. On top of this, a great portion of the bag was filled with the very rice balls and fish cakes and pickles that Mrs. Furumura had so kindly prepared and delivered the day before. 'So you won't have to cook on your last day,' she had said.

'Oh no,' thought Mother in horror, as she pictured Mrs. Furumura staring out at the forbidden mish mash of garbage. And especially, at her own lovely food that had been thoughtlessly tossed into the rubbish pile.

Mrs. Furumura smiled. She came over to Mother and patted her on the shoulder. "*Daijoubu*—it's okay," she said. "It's the least we can do. We have all really enjoyed having your family on the island. You are our guests."

The small group of people smiled and nodded in agreement. Father looked at Mother and shrugged. Mother looked at the group and then at Mrs. Furumura. She smiled helplessly.

"*Domo, domo,*" she said and gave a deep bow.

About the Author

Glenda has a particular fondness for Japan where she taught for several years at Tsuda College, an elite and historical university in Tokyo; one of the first institutions of higher education for women in Japan. While in Tokyo, Glenda and her husband adopted their first child, Taro. Glenda completed her graduate degree in Far Eastern Studies at the School of Oriental and African Studies, University of London. She spent most of her teaching career involved in international education across Canada, in Africa and Asia. Glenda speaks English, French and Japanese, and has a passion for travelling the world and learning about other cultures. She lives in West Vancouver, Canada.

www.ingramcontent.com/pod-product-compliance
Lightning Source LLC
Chambersburg PA
CBHW070601010526
44118CB00012B/1416